CONTENTS

Enid Blyton's

Tell Me a Story Book

PURNELL

ISBN 0 361 05321 5

Published 1982 by Purnell Books, Paulton, Bristol, BS18 5LQ.
Made and Printed in Great Britain by Purnell & Sons (Book Production) Limited, Paulton, Bristol.
First published by Purnell Books as *Enid Blyton's Story Book* and *Enid Blyton's Good Morning Book.*

The Fifty-pence Piece

George and Hilda were sad because Mother was ill. It was so horrid to have her in bed. Daddy looked worried too, and sighed and wished he had enough money to let Mother have cream every day and lots of fruit. But cream costs a lot of money, and so did the big purple grapes and the fine yellow pears that the doctor said would do Mother so much good.

One day Mrs. Brown gave George and Hilda fifty pence for running errands for her. They stared at it in delight. A whole fifty pence! How kind of Mrs. Brown! No one ever gave them more than ten pence—and now they had a fifty-pence piece.

''It is such a lovely bright new one,'' said George. ''It shines as if it had just been polished.''

''What shall we do with it?'' asked Hilda.

''We will buy some big yellow pears for Mother,'' said George. ''Perhaps they will help her to get better.''

''Yes, let's,'' said Hilda.

So they set off to the shops. But on the way they had an adventure.

A little boy came riding down the hill on a scooter. My goodness, it was a

fine scooter! It was painted a bright red, and it had a hooter that sounded just like the horn of a motor-car. Its wheels had tyres of good rubber, and the spokes shone like silver. It must be a new one.

"Hoot-a-toot!" went the hooter as the little boy came tearing down the hill. George and Hilda got out of the way quickly. Just as the little boy passed them a dog came running out from a gate, and the little boy went right into him. The dog yelped and ran away, not much hurt, but the little boy fell right off his scooter and bumped his head, hands, and knees hard on the ground. Something rolled out of his pocket and went down a nearby drain.

"Oh! Oh!" sobbed the little boy. "My knees are bleeding! My head is hurt! My fifty-pence piece has gone down the drain! My scooter is broken!"

George and Hilda ran to pick him up. They dusted his clothes for him and looked at his cuts.

"Come home with us and we'll bind you up and make you better," said Hilda, putting her arms round him. "Don't cry."

But the little boy wouldn't stop crying. He cried all the way to George's house. Hilda bathed his knees and hands and head, and tore up an old handkerchief for bandages. Then George had a look at the scooter. It was rather bent, but George took it to Mr. Thomas next door, and Mr. Thomas soon straightened it. It was quite all right then.

"Now, you are all nicely bound up," said Hilda. "Your knees have stopped bleeding and your scooter is mended. Stop crying, little boy, and be brave."

"But I've lost fifty pence," sobbed the little boy. "I saw it roll down the drain. I was going to buy a bell for my scooter."

"But you've got a horn," said George.

"Yes, but I want a bell too," said the little boy.

"Well, listen," said Hilda; "we have a bright new fifty-pence piece, and we'll *lend* it to you to buy a bell, but you must give us fifty pence back, because we want to buy some fruit for our mother, who is ill."

"Oh, of course I'll give it back to you," said the little boy, drying his eyes. "Please lend me your fifty-pence piece for my bell, and then I'll take you home with me and ask my father to give you another fifty pence."

So off went the three children to the toyshop, and the little boy bought a new bell with the bright new coin. He fastened it on to his scooter handle and was very pleased. "Now come home with me, and I'll ask Daddy to give you another fifty pence," he said. So the three children went up the hill together.

The little boy lived in a very large house indeed—larger than George or Hilda had ever been in before. It was quite a long way to the front door. There were enormous greenhouses on one side, and a field beyond in which two beautiful Jersey cows were eating grass. There were flowers of all kinds growing everywhere. George and Hilda felt shy.

"I don't think we'd better come in," said George. "You go and ask for fifty pence, little boy."

But before they got to the front door a big man came out from a lawn near by and said, "Hallo, Harry. What have you been doing to yourself?"

"Oh!" said the little boy. "I fell off my scooter, bang, Daddy. I cut my knees and my hands and bumped my head, and I twisted my new scooter badly and lost my fifty pence."

"And of course you howled and wept and sobbed as if you'd broken every bone in your body and lost a fortune besides!" said the big man.

"Yes, I did," said the little boy. "But these children took me home, and the little girl bathed my knees and hands and head, and tore up a handkerchief for bandages, and the little boy got my scooter mended for me—and they lent me fifty pence to buy the bell I wanted."

The big man stared in surprise at George and Hilda. "Did you really do all that?" he said. "Well, that was most kind of you. I am sure that not one of Harry's friends would do all that for him—spoilt little monkey that he is! And you even trusted him with fifty pence, though he could quite well have done without it. What were *you* going to buy with fifty pence?"

"Some big yellow pears," said Hilda shyly.

"Are you fond of pears?" asked the big man.

"Oh, they were for Mother," said George. "We earned the fifty-pence piece by running errands—it was a bright new one—and as our mother is ill and Daddy hasn't enough money to buy her the cream and the fruit that she ought to have to make her well, Hilda and I thought we could buy her some juicy pears with the fifty pence."

"Well, well, well!" said the big man. "I didn't think there were children like you in the world! Now look here, I'll make a bargain with you. Do you see those greenhouses over there? Well, they are full of grapes and peaches and nectarines. And those trees are full of pears and apples. Those Jersey cows in the field give us cream each day—and if you'll do something for me I'll send down as much fruit and cream every morning to your mother as she can manage to eat."

"Oh!" said George and Hilda, so surprised that they could hardly speak. "But what do you want us to do?"

"All I want you to do is to come and play with this spoilt boy of mine every Saturday and Sunday, and just teach him a few of the things you know—how to be brave and kind and unselfish, to begin with."

"Well," said George, "I don't think we can teach him that, you know. I mean, we shouldn't know how to."

"All right," said the man, "just come and play with him. He'll learn lots of things from you, without you worrying your heads about anything. Is that a bargain, then?"

"Yes, thank you," said George and Hilda. And then such lovely things happened. The big man took them into a greenhouse and cut a large bunch of purple

grapes. He picked a basketful of peaches and nectarines. He sent to the kitchen for a jug of cream. He picked four large red apples from the trees. And then he put them all into a car, and drove the two children home himself!

Wasn't it lovely? Hilda and George kept their part of the bargain. They went to play with Harry each Saturday and Sunday, and they had a very fine time, for Harry's garden was marvellous for Red Indians and hide-and-seek and things like that. And Harry's father sent down fruit and cream to the children's mother each day, and in a few weeks' time she was strong and well and was running about just as merrily as she used to do.

And Harry became a much nicer little boy. He learnt to share things with Hilda and George. He learnt to be brave and not howl when he fell down. He learnt to be kind.

"It was a very good thing for everybody that you fell down that day," George said to Harry.

"Yes, it was," said Harry, giving George and Hilda a big hug. "You are the best friends I ever had."

The Inquisitive Hedgehog

There was once a most inquisitive hedgehog, who liked to know everybody else's business. He used to shuffle round the ditches, listening to all that the toad said to the frog, and trying to find out where the squirrel had hidden his winter nuts.

The pixies who lived in the hedgerows were most annoyed with him, for he was always trying to find out their secrets, and, as you know, pixies have many magic secrets which no one but themselves must know. Whenever they met together to talk they had to be sure to look under the dead leaves or behind the ivy to see if Prickles the hedgehog was hiding there ready to listen.

Now, one day a wizard called Tonks came to visit the pixie Lightfoot, who lived in a small house in the bank of the hedgerow. This house had a little door overhung with a curtain of green moss, so that no one could see it when passing by.

Inside the door was a cosy room, set with little tables, chairs, and couches, for Lightfoot often had parties and needed plenty of furniture. There was a small fireplace at one end, and on it Lightfoot boiled his kettle and fried his bacon.

Tonks was to come and have a very important talk with Lightfoot and the other pixies about the party that was to be given in honour of the Fairy Princess's birthday the next winter. Prickles overheard the toad telling the little brown mouse, and he longed to know what day the party was to be, and if the creatures of the hedgerows were to be invited as well as the fairy folk.

But nobody could tell him, for nobody knew. "Nothing is decided yet," said the toad; "and even when it is I don't suppose *we* shall know until the invitations are sent, Prickles. You must just be patient."

"Yes, but, you see, I want to go and visit my grandmother, who lives far away on the hillside," said Prickles. "And if I choose a week when the party is held it would be most unfortunate."

"Well, we shan't miss you very much," said the toad, going under his stone. He was not at all fond of the inquisitive hedgehog.

Prickles wondered and wondered how he could get to know what the pixies would say when Tonks the wizard came to talk with them. And at last he thought of an idea.

"If I creep into Lightfoot's house just before the pixies and the wizard go there to meet, and cover myself with a cloth, I shall look like a sofa or a big stool, and no one will notice me. Then I can lie quietly under my cloth and hear everything," he thought to himself. "What a good idea!"

So he borrowed a red shawl from the old brownie woman who lived in the hazel-copse, and stuffed it into a hole in the bank, where an old wasps' nest had once been. Then he waited impatiently for the evening to come when Tonks was to see the hedgerow pixies.

At last it came. Prickles took his shawl out of the hole and went to where the green moss-curtain hung over Lightfoot's little door. As he crouched there, looking like a brown clod of earth, the door opened, and Lightfoot ran out. He was going to fetch some cakes. He left his door open, and Prickles quickly went inside.

The room was neatly arranged with chairs and stools in a circle. Prickles pushed them about and made room for himself. He threw the red shawl over his prickly back and crouched down, looking like a couch without a back, or a great stool. He was pleased. Now he could hear everything.

Very soon Lightfoot came back. He was humming a little tune, as he put out the cakes neatly on a dish and set the kettle on the fire to boil water for some tea.

Presently there was a knocking at the door. Lightfoot opened it. In came the pixies from the hedgerow, chattering and laughing.

''Find seats for yourselves,'' said Lightfoot. ''I'm just making the tea. I've some cakes, too, if you like to help yourselves.''

''We'll wait till old Wizard Tonks comes,'' said the pixies. They sat down on the chairs and began to talk. Prickles listened hard with both his ears, hoping to hear a few secrets.

Rat-tat-tat! Someone knocked loudly on the door. It was Tonks the wizard. Lightfoot ran to open it, and bowed the old wizard into the cosy room.

''Good evening, everyone,'' said Tonks. He was a round, fat wizard, with white hair and a white beard that was so long he had to keep it tied up in a big knot or he would have tripped over it.

''Good evening!'' cried the pixies, and they all stood up, for the wizard was a wise old fellow and everyone respected him.

''Well!'' said Tonks, taking off his long black cloak. ''We have come to

discuss a most important matter together—the party for the Fairy Princess this winter.''

''Won't you have a nice cup of hot tea before you begin the meeting?'' asked Lightfoot, coming up with a big cup of steaming-hot tea. ''Sit down and make yourself comfortable, Tonks.''

Tonks looked round for a seat. He was fat and rather heavy, so he chose the biggest seat he could see, which, as you will guess, was Prickles the hedgehog under his red shawl!

Tonks sat down heavily, holding his cup of tea in his right hand and a cake in his left.

But no sooner had he sat down than he shot up again in a fearful hurry, shouting, ''Oh! Ooooh! Ow! Pins and needles! What is it? Ooooooh!''

He was so scared at sitting down on the prickly hedgehog that he upset his hot tea all over the two pixies who were sitting next to him. His cake flew up into the air and hit Lightfoot on the head when it came down! Dear, dear, what a commotion there was, to be sure!

"What's the matter, what's the matter?" everyone cried.

"Ooooooh!" said the poor wizard, rubbing himself hard, for the hedgehog was very, very prickly, and all the prickles had pricked Tonks when he sat down so hard.

"Oooooooh!" said the two pixies who had been scalded by the tea.

"Ooooh!" said Lightfoot, wondering what had hit him.

"How dare you put pins and needles on the seat left for me?" roared Tonks suddenly, shaking his fist in Lightfoot's face. "How dare you, I say?"

"Whatever do you mean?" said Lightfoot, most astonished. "Don't talk to me like that, please, Tonks. I don't like it. And, anyway, what do *you* mean by throwing your nice hot tea over my friends?"

Prickles began to think he was going to get into trouble. Se he began to move quietly towards the door, but a pixie saw him and shrieked with fright.

"Look at that sofa! It's walking! Oh, look at it! It's gone magic!"

All the pixies looked at what they thought was a sofa walking towards the door. Tonks looked too.

"Why, that's the sofa I sat down on!" he cried. "It was as prickly as could be! Catch it! Quick! Catch it!"

Prickles was very frightened. He ran towards the door, and just as he reached it a pixie pulled at the red shawl he had thrown over himself.

"Oh! It's Prickles, the inquisitive hedgehog!" cried Lightfoot angrily. "He came here and hid himself to hear our secrets. No wonder poor Tonks thought he was sitting on pins and needles! Catch him!"

But Prickles was safely out of the door. He banged it behind him and scurried off through the ditch. He made his way through the stinging-nettles, and ran to a hole in the bank that he knew very well. A big stone covered the entrance and a fern grew over the stone. He would hide there!

Tonks, Lightfoot, and all the other pixies raced after him. They did not like stinging-nettles, so they went round them, and by the time they had got to the other side Prickles was nowhere to be seen.

"Find him, find him!" raged Tonks. "I'll teach him to prick me! Yes, I will! I'll make him eat a dinner of needles cooked in hot tea! I'll pull out all his prickles! I'll—I'll—I'll——"

Prickles heard all that Tonks was saying, and he trembled in his hole. He was

safe there, and the stone and fern hid him well. He did hope that no one would find him.

No one did. The pixies hunted for a long time, and then gave it up.

"He must have gone to his grandmother on the hillside," said Lightfoot. "Let's go back."

"Now listen!" said Tonks fiercely. "You keep a look-out for that rascal of a hedgehog all the winter. As soon as he shows his nose bring him to me! I'll keep a fine meal of cooked needles for him! I'll be going away to Dreamland in the springtime, so find him before that.''

''Yes, Tonks,'' said the pixies. ''We are always about this hedgerow, so we are sure to see him. Anyway, he will come to the party; we'll catch him then.''

Prickles heard, and how he trembled when he heard of the cooked needles!

''I shan't get out of this hole until Tonks goes to Dreamland,'' he decided.

So all that winter Prickles kept in his little hole. He did not go out to catch beetles or slugs, but just curled himself up and slept soundly. He only awoke one night when he heard a noise of laughing and chattering—and when he poked his nose out he found that it was the party that was being given in honour of the Princess's birthday! Poor Prickles! He didn't dare to go to it and he saw the rabbit, the hare, the squirrel and the little brown mouse all hopping and running along to have a good time, but he had to keep close to his hole.

It really served him right, didn't it? And, do you know, it's a strange thing, but ever since that winter hedgehogs have always slept through the cold days! Perhaps they are still afraid of Tonks! I shouldn't be surprised.

The Quarrelsome Brownies

Snippy and Snappy were two brownies who lived next door to each other. They were bad-tempered fellows, always quarrelling, and yet they always did everything together if they possibly could.

"Let's go blackberrying today, Snippy," said Snappy one morning.

"Very well," said Snippy. "*I* shall make a blackberry pudding."

"Oh, a blackberry tart is *much* nicer," said Snappy.

"No, a pudding is better," said Snippy. "You get lots of juice in a pudding, but if you make an open tart of blackberries you don't get any juice."

They quarrelled all the way to the woods about puddings and tarts—and then they began to pick their blackberries. They each had a big basket. The blackberries were very ripe and black, and they were as sweet as could be. Both brownies soon had black mouths, for they ate as many as they put in their baskets!

"I've got enough," said Snippy. "I shall go home."

"No; wait for me," said Snappy. "I want some more."

Snippy put his basket down on the ground and wandered off to look for nuts. Snappy went on picking fast—and as he picked he came nearer and nearer to Snippy's basket. He didn't see it, for he had his back to it.

Snippy, coming back from his search for nuts, suddenly yelled to Snappy.

"Hi! Look where you are putting your big feet! You'll upset my basket!"

Snappy jumped in fright, and his foot went into Snippy's basket. It upset—and all his blackberries rolled on the ground!

"Oh, you careless, careless brownie!" shouted Snippy, in a rage. "Look at that!"

"Well, pick them up, then," said Snappy. "It was your own fault, shouting at me like that and making me jump. How was I to know I'd jump right into your silly basket?"

"It isn't a silly basket," roared Snippy. "It's better than yours. And how can I pick up my blackberries when they have rolled over an ants' nest and ants are nibbling them all?"

"They won't hurt you," said Snappy.

"You just give me some of *your* blackberries!" cried Snippy, and he ran at Snappy. But the brownie was too quick for him, and tore off through the woods

with his basket. Snippy stopped, out of breath. He knew he would never catch Snappy. He went back to his blackberries.

''Oh, dear!'' he groaned in dismay. ''Now the wasps have found them too. I really daren't pick them up. I'd pick up handfuls of ants and wasps as well. They'll have to stay there. Bother Snappy! He'll have a fine blackberry tart, and I won't have my blackberry pudding, after all!''

Snippy picked up his empty basket and went slowly home. The more he thought about Snappy's blackberry tart the angrier he became.

''I've a good mind to creep into Snappy's kitchen and see if I can take *his* blackberries,'' thought Snippy. ''He upset mine, so why shouldn't I have his?''

When he got home he poked his nose over the wall to see what Snappy was doing. He heard him banging about in the kitchen, so he knew it was no use going to get the blackberries then. He would wait till it was dark.

And what was Snappy doing? He was so afraid that Snippy might come to take away his blackberries that he was busy cooking them already! He had made some lovely pastry, and had cooked the blackberries with plenty of sugar. He took the tart out of the oven—a beautiful tart, big, delicious, and spread so thickly with blackberries that really there was hardly any pastry to be seen!

"Aha!" said Snappy to himself. "There's a fine tart! Snippy is silly to say that a blackberry pudding is better than a tart. He's quite wrong. If he hadn't been so horrid to me I might have given him a piece, but I shan't now."

Snappy put the beautiful tart on the bottom shelf of the larder to cool. He thought he would have some for supper that night.

"But it would be nice to have some cream with it," said Snappy. "I'll just run out and ask Dame Cheese for a jug of cream."

So out he went, carrying his little lantern, for by now it was getting dark. Snippy heard the front door bang, and he grinned. Now was the time to steal into Snappy's kitchen and take away his basket of blackberries! Snippy didn't guess that Snappy

had made them into a tart already.

He climbed over the wall. He pushed up the window and slipped inside. It was quite dark in the kitchen, and as Snippy didn't dare to light a candle he had to feel about in the dark for the blackberries.

He felt on the table. Nothing there. He felt on the dresser. Nothing there, either. He felt on the shelf. No, no blackberries there. They must be in the larder. He opened the larder door. He felt about the shelves. He couldn't find any basket on the bottom shelf—nor on the next shelf—nor on the next one. Snippy couldn't reach the highest one of all, and he felt sure that Snappy must have put the blackberries there—no doubt about it!

''Well, I can get up there if I stand on the bottom shelf,'' said Snippy, quite determined to get those blackberries! So he stood on the bottom shelf, and felt eagerly on the highest one with his hand.

And just as he was doing that he heard the front door open. It was Snappy who had come back again! Oh, dear, dear, dear! Snippy got such a shock that he

slipped and fell. He sat down BANG on the bottom shelf, and—would you believe it?—although he didn't know it, he had sat right down in the middle of that lovely juicy blackberry tart. He had, really!

Snappy heard the bang in the larder. It frightened him.

"What a large mouse that must be," he said, trembling. He lighted his candle and went to look, and to his great surprise he saw Snippy in his larder, looking very much ashamed of himself.

"Snippy! Have you come to steal my tart?" cried Snappy. He flashed his candle round the larder. "Oh, you have, you have! It's gone! Have you eaten it?"

"I *haven't* taken your tart," said Snippy. "I haven't even tasted it. I came for your blackberries. You spoilt mine, so I thought you ought to give me yours."

"Where is my tart, my beautiful blackberry tart?" cried Snappy, in despair. "Even the dish has gone!"

Now you can guess where the blackberry tart was—sticking tightly to Snippy's trousers! So was the dish—but Snippy didn't know it.

"I'll help you to look for the tart," he said to Snappy. But no matter where the two of them looked they could see no sign of the blackberry tart! Snippy sat down on a chair at last, and looked quite startled to hear the clang that the enamelled dish made as he sat down.

Suddenly Snappy gave a shriek. "Look! Look! Snippy, you are dripping ink all over the place! Oh, my nice carpet! Is your fountain-pen leaking?"

Snippy took it out of his pocket to see. No, it was quite all right. He looked down at the black drops all over the carpet in the greatest astonishment. How could he be leaking ink?

And then he felt behind himself—and he found the dish of blackberry tart there, sticking tightly to his trousers, dripping rich black juice everywhere!

"Snappy," said Snippy in a small voice, "I know where your tart is."

"Where?" asked Snappy, looking all round.

"I'm sitting on it," said Snippy. "I must have fallen right into it in the larder, and didn't know."

He got up and turned himself round—and Snappy saw his blackberry tart there. He looked as black as thunder at first, and then his mouth tilted upwards—and he began to laugh—and laugh—and laugh!

"Oh, Snippy, you do look funny!" he said. "And, dear me, how strange—I *trod* on your blackberries by mistake, and now you've *sat* on mine! We are even, Snippy, so let's stop quarrelling and go blackberrying again tomorrow."

"What about my lovely new trousers?" wailed Snippy, trying to wipe the tart off. ‘‘They are quite, quite spoilt.’’

‘‘Well, you shouldn’t have come sneaking into my larder,’’ said Snappy. ‘‘I really think that serves you right.’’

‘‘You horrid, mean, unkind thing!’’ cried Snippy; and in another moment both the quarrelsome little brownies were squabbling as hard as could be. They picked up bits of the blackberry tart and threw them hard at one another. Squish! Squish! What a mess there was!

It took Snappy the whole morning to clean up his kitchen next day; and it took Snippy the whole morning to wash his nice new trousers.

They went off to the woods to find some more blackberries in the afternoon—but whether they will manage to make puddings and tarts of them this time I don’t know! What do *you* think?

The Party in the Hollow Tree

John was very good at climbing trees. He could climb every tree in his garden except one little apple-tree that was too small to bear his weight.

"I'm tired of climbing trees in the garden," John said to his sister Polly one day. "I'd like to climb some big trees out in the wood. Would you like to come with me? You can't climb them, but you can watch me."

"All right," said Polly. She wasn't at all good at climbing, but she loved to hear John say what he could see from the top of the trees he climbed. So off they went one sunny afternoon into the wood.

First John climbed this tree, then that tree. He told Polly that from the top of the first tree he could see Farmer Giles' cows far away in the meadow, standing up to their knees in the stream to cool themselves. Polly wished she could see them too, but she knew she would never be able to climb to the top branch as John did.

From the top of the next tree John could see Mrs. Jones hanging out the washing in her garden down the hill. That was a very long way to see.

And from the top of the next tree—but wait a minute, that was the funny old hollow tree that was so surprising inside!

John climbed up it, not knowing that it was hollow, for it was so big and sturdy-looking. He got halfway up and then happened to look down. And he saw that the tree was quite hollow inside, so hollow that there seemed to be a little room there, round and dark.

And in that little room there was a small table with four little chairs set round it! On the table was a yellow cloth with a border, and set on the cloth was a meal! There were four blue plates, four blue cups and saucers with little silver spoons, a plate of brown bread and butter, a pot of jam, a plate of chocolate cakes, and a teapot and jug of milk. John was so astonished that he nearly fell down the tree!

"What can you see from the top of that tree, John?" asked Polly, peering upwards.

"I say, Polly! What do you think? This tree is hollow inside and I can see such a funny thing!"

"What?" asked Polly.

"I can see a table laid for tea, and four little chairs set round it," said John.

"I don't believe you," said Polly. "You're just making it up."

"I'm *not!*" cried John. "I'm not! It's perfectly true. What a pity you can't come up and see it! Oh, Polly, I wonder who's going to go to the tea-party inside this tree. I'd love to see."

"I don't believe you one bit," said Polly. "I'm sure you're just pretending, to make me sorry I can't climb as well as you can."

"No, I'm not, I tell you," said John. "Oh, Polly, do believe me. We've often wanted to see fairies, and now, if only you'll be quiet, I believe we shall be able to see some. Hide under a bush, there's a good girl, and watch to see who comes to this tree. I expect there's a secret door to it somewhere."

So Polly went to hide, and John sat as still as a mouse up in the tree, peeping downwards to where the tea-table was set in the hollow below.

Suddenly, from out of a tiny trap-door behind one of the chairs, a small gnome appeared. John could hardly believe his eyes. Then another one came, and then two more. They all took their places at the little table, and began to eat their tea.

As they ate they talked. John could hear quite plainly what they said. They were talking about a dance that the Fairy Queen was giving that very night.

"It's to be under the gorse bush that grows highest up the hill," said one gnome, eating a piece of bread and butter very quickly.

"What time?" asked the gnome next to him, pouring out a cup of very strong tea.

"When the Moon looks through the fir trees yonder," said the first gnome. "Pass me a cake, please."

"Do you know, I feel as if humans were somewhere about," said the third gnome, solemnly.

"Yes, I feel a bit uncomfortable too," said the last one, drinking his tea rather noisily. "But there's nobody near us, I'm sure."

And at that very moment John's nose began to tickle dreadfully, and, oh, dear

me, he gave a most *enormous* sneeze! A-TISHOO! Then another—A-TISHOO!

The gnomes leapt up from the little table and gazed upwards through the branches. When they saw John they gave a shout of dismay, clapped their hands loudly together, and vanished completely. The table disappeared too, and all the chairs. There wasn't a thing to be seen!

John was so upset. He hoped the gnomes would come back, but they didn't. So he called Polly and told her all he had seen.

But Polly just *wouldn't* believe him! She thought he was making it all up again. John was quite angry with her, but it wasn't a bit of use. She hadn't seen the gnomes herself nor the tea-table, and she thought it was all make-believe.

"Well, I'm going to climb right down inside the hollow part, and see if I can find anything that the gnomes left," said John, crossly. "I never knew such a disbeliever as you, Polly."

So he carefully lowered himself down inside the tree and looked round. At first he could see nothing at all except cobwebs—and then he saw something shining white on the ground. He picked it up.

It was a square card, quite small, and on it was printed an invitation.

To the Hollow-Tree Gnomes.
Please Come to a Dance
On Full-Moon Night,
By Invitation of the Fairy Queen

"There!" cried John, in glee. "They've dropped their invitation-card. Now Polly will have to believe me!"

He climbed out of the tree and showed her the card. She really did believe his story then, and looked tremendously excited.

"Oh, John, I'm sorry I thought you were making it all up," she said. "Do you think—oh, do you think we might creep out tonight and hide somewhere to watch the dance?"

"Yes, we will!" said John, in great excitement. "Oh, Polly, what fun! We'll hide under the next gorse bush to the highest one on the hill; then we shall see and hear beautifully."

I do wonder what they'll see, don't you? They're going tonight, and taking the gnomes' card with them, so that if they see the gnomes again they can return the card and ask whether they may join in the dance too.

I expect they will be allowed to—and I *do* wish you and I were going too!

Pip and the Badger

"Pip!" called Aunt Twinkle, "it's Saturday and I'm busy. Will you go and do my shopping for me?"

"Yes, Aunt," said Pip; "but I hope I don't have to stand in many queues. It's so cold!"

"Well, put on your new scarf and your woolly coat," said Aunt Twinkle. "Here's the basket and my shopping list. Now, off you go!"

Pip went off rather gloomily. He thought he would go through the wood because he might meet one of his friends, Sandy the rabbit, there.

But he didn't meet Sandy. He met somebody else! He was passing an ivy-covered bank when he heard a queer snorting noise. Whatever could it be?

Some leaves and sand came flying from the bank and then Pip saw a striped, black-and-white head peeping out of a hole. It was a big head, and it made Pip jump with fright. He turned to run away.

"Wait, wait!" called a gruff voice. "What are you frightened of, you silly? I'm only Brock the badger."

"Oh!" said Pip, stopping. "Of course—you've been asleep all the winter, haven't you? Are you going to wake up now and come out and play?"

"I don't know," said the badger. "I want to know what date it is, first."

"Well, it's Saturday, February the first," said Pip. "But why do you want to know the date?"

"For a very good reason!" said the badger. "Didn't you know that on the *second* of February I poke my nose out of my den to see what the weather's like? If it is warm and the grass is green I go back to sleep again, because I know there still is bitter weather to come. But if the snow is on the ground and the frost is about, I wake up properly and come out. I know that the winter is over, you see. Don't you know the old rhyme:

'If Candlemas Day be fair and bright,
Winter will have another flight;
But if Candlemas Day be clouds and rain,
Winter has gone and will not come again.' "

"Well, that seems queer to me," said Pip. "You're a day early, Brock. It's tomorrow you have to poke your nose out. Go back! I just hope that the snow is on the ground when you look out tomorrow; then we'll know that the spring will soon be here!"

The badger went back into his den. He will be poking his nose out tomorrow to see what the weather is like. Let's hope that the snow is on the ground, then spring will be just round the corner! Wise old fellow, the badger, isn't he?

The House Made of Cards

Wendy and Jack had built a lovely house out of their snap cards. First they put two cards leaning together—then they put one on each side—then they put two on top of the side ones, resting on them, and built another room on top of that. You know how to do it, don't you?

They made such a high house. Really, they had never made such a tall card-house before. It was a perfectly lovely one. Wendy called Mother and she cried out in surprise.

''Well, you certainly have built a fine house this time,'' she said.

''Could we leave it on the table till the morning?'' asked Jack. ''It seems a shame to knock it down tonight.''

''Well, leave it there,'' said Mother. ''You can see it tomorrow morning then. I won't touch it when I do the room before breakfast.''

So the two children left their card-house on the table. How high it was!

That night, when all was dark in the playroom except for the flicker of the fire in the grate, a pixie came hurrying out of a mousehole where he had been hiding. He was looking for a house to live in. He looked into the dolls' house, but the dolls wouldn't let him in.

"We know you, Mister Grabby," they said. "You'd take the best bed to sleep in, the most comfortable chair to sit in, and the nicest cake out of the oven. No, thank you! We don't want you here. Go and look for somewhere else to live."

Mister Grabby, the pixie, made a rude face at the dolls and wandered off. Then suddenly he saw the lovely house of cards on the table.

"My!" he said. "That's a fine house! I wonder if anyone lives there? If nobody does, I shall live there myself. Shan't I be grand? I wonder how many rooms it has?"

He walked into the house of cards. Dear me, it had ten rooms! Would you believe it? Grabby was delighted. He had never had such a grand house before.

He took his tiny magic wand and waved it. He meant to make chairs, tables, and beds by magic, and he was just going to say the right words when he heard a little voice calling to him.

"Mister Grabby! Is this your house?"

Grabby hurried down the stairs and outside to see who was speaking. It was the little mouse in whose hole he had been hiding all that day.

"Yes, this is my house," he said grandly. "What do you want?"

"Well, Mister Grabby, that old black cat has come into the playroom tonight and she's sitting near my hole," said the mouse. "I daren't go back there. So I thought you would perhaps give me shelter in your grand house for tonight."

"I can't," said the selfish pixie. "I want all the rooms myself. I don't want any mice here."

"Oh, Mister Grabby," said the tiny mouse, "how unkind of you! Didn't I share my hole with you when you asked me yesterday? Please share your house with me till the cat goes away."

"I tell you I won't!" said Grabby crossly. "Go away and be eaten! You're a nuisance!"

Now, that made the mouse feel very angry indeed. He made up his mind that he *would* sleep in the house of cards that night. So when Grabby had gone upstairs he crept in at the bottom of it and lay down to sleep. But the pixie knew he was there and came flying down in a rage. He hit the mouse with his wand.

"Ow!" cried the mouse, and climbed quickly into the room above. The pixie flew after him. Up went the mouse and scrambled into another room. The pixie followed, shouting out in a dreadful temper.

The pixie hit the mouse whenever he could, and soon the tiny creature was full of bruises. He thought that the selfish pixie was the most horrible fellow he had ever met.

"I wish I hadn't shared my hole with you," he squeaked, as he ran in and out of one room after another. "I wish I hadn't! I wish I hadn't."

Poor little mouse! The pixie caught him at last and gave him such a whipping with his magic wand. The little mouse wept tears all down the cards. Then he crept away to the end of the table and washed his face, thinking hard all the time.

''That pixie wants punishing!'' said the mouse. ''He's selfish and unkind. I share my things with others—so why shouldn't he? I shall punish him.''

He watched the pixie climb into the topmost room of the house of cards. He saw him take a handkerchief out of his pocket to polish up his magic wand.

''I shall go and nibble away his house at the bottom,'' said the mouse to himself. ''Yes, that's what I will do.''

So, as soon as the pixie had forgotten all about him, he crept back to the house and began to nibble at a card with his sharp teeth!

Soon the card was gnawed almost through. It dropped flat on the table, for it could no longer stand upright. And as soon as it dropped, all the house of cards came tumbling down.

Flip, flap, flip, flap! Down it came, and the cards swished softly into a heap on the table. There was no house left. How astonished that pixie was! He tumbled down with the cards and bumped his head.

''Oh, oh,'' he cried in a fright. ''What is happening? It's an earthquake! I must fly away quickly!''

He spread his wings and flew away, quite forgetting to take his little magic wand with him. It lay under the cards. The mouse didn't see it, either. He chuckled to himself when he saw what a fright the pixie was in.

"Serves him right," he said. "And see! The noise of the cards falling has frightened away the cat! I can go back to my hole in safety."

Back he went, and all was quiet in the playroom until the children came in the next morning.

"Oh, look!" cried Jack. "Our lovely house of cards has fallen down. And what is this—a card nibbled quite in half! A mouse must have done that—but I wonder why!"

Wendy picked up the cards—and suddenly she found the tiny magic wand.

"Look at this," she said to Jack. "What is it? It looks like a silver match-stick with a star at the end!"

"Oh, it's a magic wand!" said Jack. "Let's use it and see what happens."

But before they could wish anything Mother called them to go and get ready for school. Wasn't it a pity?

"Never mind, we'll use it tonight after tea," said Wendy.

I do wish I was going to be there, don't you?

Midnight Tea-party

I peeped one night in the playroom,
And I was surprised to see
The golly and the teddy
Having their friends to tea!

The clockwork mouse and old Jumbo,
The sailor doll and the clown,
And all the dolls from the dolls' house
At the table were sitting down.

Golly had borrowed my tea-set,
And Teddy was cutting a cake.
There were jellies a-shake in the dishes,
And crackers for each one to take.

You think I was dreaming? I wasn't!
Today I found crumbs on the mat,
And jelly in one of the dishes,
And the golly's striped paper hat!

Treacle-pudding Town

Thomas loved treacle pudding. His mother would often make a great big one for her four children, with golden syrup poured all over it. Thomas thought it was the nicest pudding in the world.

He was greedy. He ate up his slice of pudding as quickly as he could, so that he could have a second helping before anyone else did.

''Don't gobble, Thomas,'' his mother said. But as he gobbled because he wanted to have more than anybody else, he just went on gobbling.

He gobbled his bread-and-butter at tea-time so that he could have more cakes than anybody, especially if there was a chocolate cake. The other children were cross with him. ''It isn't fair,'' they said. ''You are greedy, Thomas, and you always try to have more than your fair share!''

One day there was a fine treacle pudding for dinner. Thomas had two big helpings—and then his mother said the rest of the pudding was to be saved for Ellen,

his sister, who was going to be late for dinner that day. Thomas watched his mother put it into the larder. He longed and longed for just another piece, although he had really had quite enough.

His mother went out into the garden to put some clothes on the line. Thomas opened the larder door and peeped inside. There was the rest of the treacle pudding, still on the dish, warm and sticky! Thomas looked and looked at it.

And then, what do you think he did? He stole up to the shelf, took a spoon and gobbled up the rest of that pudding.

Wasn't he horrid? When he had finished it all, he was frightened. What would his mother say? What would his sister do? She would smack him hard and pull his hair, because when she flew into a temper she was very rough.

Thomas ran down the garden, squeezed through the hedge at the bottom, and sat in the field there.

"I do wish I needn't go home again," he said to himself. "I *shall* get into trouble when I do!"

He sighed a heavy sigh, and a small man hurrying by stopped and looked at him in surprise.

"What's the matter?" he asked.

"Oh, I just don't want to go back home," said Thomas. "I'm afraid I shall be smacked if I do."

"Poor boy!" said the little man. He had a long beard reaching nearly to his toes, and the brightest eyes that Thomas had ever seen. "Well, why go home? Isn't there somewhere else you can go?"

"No," said Thomas. "But oh, how I wish I could go to some place where I could have treacle pudding and chocolate cake, as much as ever I liked! I never have enough at home."

"Dear, dear!" said the little man. He was a brownie, though Thomas didn't know this. "Well, I think I can help you. What about coming with me to Treacle-Pudding Town? It's not very far."

Thomas could hardly believe his ears. Treacle-Pudding Town! What a wonderful place it sounded. He jumped up at once.

"I'll go," he said. "Is there really plenty of treacle pudding there?"

"Oh, yes," said the brownie, "and chocolate cake too. It's a famous place for that, you know. They do nothing there but make and sell treacle puddings and chocolate cake. My cousin lives there. I'll take you to stay with him if you like. He'll be pleased to have you."

Well, greedy little Thomas was only too pleased to go. He forgot that his mother would worry about him. He forgot that he was supposed to go to school that afternoon.

He just wanted to get to those puddings and cakes. So off he went with the brownie.

He went across the field, over the stile, and into the wood. And in the very middle of the wood was Treacle-Pudding Town! Thomas stood and stared at it. It was a most extraordinary place.

"Why, the houses are the shape of treacle puddings and chocolate cakes!" he said. "How funny! And look at that stream—I'm sure it's full of treacle instead of water."

"Here is my cousin's house," said the brownie, going into a tiny house shaped like a birthday cake. The chimneys looked like three candles smoking!

"Tippy, Tippy, are you in?" cried the brownie. "I've brought a friend to stay with you."

"Very pleased to have him, I'm sure," said Tippy, who was a little man very like his cousin. He smelt of chocolate. In fact, the whole village smelt of chocolate and treacle. Thomas liked it.

"Well, goodbye, Thomas," said the first brownie. "I hope you'll have a good time. You can eat as much as ever you like here, you know."

Thomas was so excited. "Can I really?" he said. "I didn't have much dinner. Can I have some treacle pudding?"

"Certainly," said Tippy. He went to the kitchen and came back with a white dish in which was a steaming hot pudding with yellow treacle poured all over it. "Help yourself. I don't want any."

Well, you may not believe it, but Thomas ate all that treacle pudding! Tippy saw the empty dish and grinned.

"I've another pudding in the kitchen," he said. "Will you have it?"

But, dear me, Thomas felt as if he couldn't eat even a small slice. He shook his head. "I feel as if I want to go to sleep," he said.

"I should think so," said Tippy. He showed Thomas a couch, and the little boy lay down on it. He slept till tea-time. Then he woke up. He smelt chocolate cakes baking and was glad.

"Hallo!" said Tippy, coming in to lay the tea-table. "Tea-time! New cakes!"

Thomas got up and sat at the table. Tippy put three plates on the table—one had small chocolate buns on it, one had a round chocolate cake, and one had a square one.

"Ha! No bread-and-butter!" said Thomas, pleased.

"Oh, no," said Tippy. "Just cakes. Help yourself. I don't want any."

Thomas thought it was funny not to want any. Anyway, that left all the more

for him! He ate all the little buns. He ate half the round chocolate cake and then he began on the square one. But, oh dear, what a pity! Before he was halfway through it, he suddenly felt as if he didn't want any more! What a waste of cake! He drank his tea and went out into the street.

All the shops sold treacle puddings and chocolate cakes—nothing else at all! Thomas looked into two or three windows and then he got rather bored with seeing the same things, and wished he could find a toyshop. But there wasn't one.

He found some brownie children and played with them for a long time. They liked him, and asked him to go back to their home to have supper with them.

Thomas was feeling hungry again. It was a long time since tea-time. He went to their house, wondering what there would be for supper.

What do you suppose it was? Yes—a great big treacle pudding. Thomas stared at it. He wasn't so pleased to see it as he had been to see the one at dinner-time. But, all the same, he managed to eat two helpings of it. Then he went back to Tippy's house and undressed to go bed.

In the morning he was very hungry again. He wondered if there would be bacon or kippers or eggs for breakfast, and perhaps porridge and toast and marmalade. Lovely! He ran downstairs.

But, good gracious, Tippy brought in a treacle pudding for breakfast! Thomas was really disappointed.

"You don't look pleased to see my beautiful pudding," said Tippy, offended. "Well, there's nothing else. I haven't baked any chocolate cakes yet. Eat up your pudding."

So Thomas ate it all up, but somehow he didn't enjoy it. He was getting very tired of treacle pudding. And he was even more tired of it when dinner-time came and he found that there was nothing but chocolate buns and treacle pudding again. He felt as if he really *couldn't* eat any!

"If only it was rice pudding or stewed apples!" said Thomas to Tippy.

Tippy looked as cross as could be. "You horrid, ungrateful boy!" he said.

''What did you want to come to Treacle-Pudding Town for? My cousin said you were a very greedy boy, and would love to eat as much as I could cook for you—and now, the very first dinner-time you are here, you turn up your nose at my nice pudding. Eat it up at once, I tell you!''

''I can't!'' said poor Thomas. ''Somehow it looks horrid to me now, that treacle pudding!''

''Horrid?'' cried Tippy. ''How dare you say that about my treacle pudding?''

Tippy was very angry. He picked up the treacle pudding and threw it straight at Thomas. It hit him on the nose and the treacle ran down his face. Then Tippy snowballed him with the chocolate buns. Thomas ran out of the house, crying. He was very unhappy and wanted his mother.

''Help, Mummy!'' he shouted.

He ran through the town. He ran through the wood. He climbed over the stile and ran across the field back to his home. He rushed up to his mother, who was baking chocolate cakes.

''Mother! Mother!'' cried Thomas, hugging her. ''Did you wonder where I had been all this time?''

''No, Thomas,'' said his mother in surprise. ''It is only an hour since dinner.''

Then Thomas knew that a day in Treacle-Pudding Town was only an hour in our world, and he was glad. But there was something he had to tell his mother.

"Mother," he said, "please forgive me—but I ate the rest of the treacle pudding out of the larder."

"Oh, Thomas, how naughty of you!" said his mother, shocked. "It's a good thing that Ellen has stayed to dinner at school, after all. You must never do such a thing again—but I will forgive you, because you have told me. Thomas, don't be a greedy little boy—no one likes greedy children."

"I won't any more," promised Thomas.

"I expect you will be, though, at tea-time, when you see new chocolate buns on the table!" said his mother.

But she got a surprise, for Thomas wouldn't eat a single chocolate bun! And he won't eat treacle pudding, either! He can't bear to see one on the table. His mother doesn't know why, so she can't understand it—but I know why Thomas has changed, don't you?

Mary Jane, the Little Doll

Joan had a fine dolls' house. There were two rooms downstairs, two rooms on the first floor, and three rooms on the top floor. So she was able to have a kitchen and a dining-room, a drawing-room and a nursery, and three little bedrooms at the top. It really was a beautiful house.

Joan had saved up her money each week and bought furniture for her house, and now at last every room had its chairs, tables, beds, or chests. She had made little curtains for the windows, and had laid strips of carpet on the floors.

''Well,'' said Joan, looking into the dolls' house one morning, ''you do look a pretty little house. You are quite ready for some little dolls to live in. See, little house, here are the people who will live in you now.''

Joan walked a little lady doll into the house and sat her on a chair. Then she walked a little gentleman doll in and stood him by the dining-room mantelpiece. Then came three little girl and boy dolls and a little doll dressed as a nanny. Those went upstairs to the nursery. It did look nice to see such a lot of dolls in the little house. It made it seem so real.

Joan's mummy came in to see the dolls' house, and she thought it was lovely.

"You ought to have a nice little maid doll in the kitchen!" she said. "Shall I dress you one this afternoon, Joan?"

"Oh, do, Mummy!" cried Joan.

So Mummy cut out a dear little blue frock and a little white apron and cap, and she dressed a small doll in them.

The little doll looked very smart indeed. Joan was pleased with her. She put her in the kitchen by the little stove.

"I shall call you Mary Jane," she said. "Mummy's home-help is called Mary Jane, and she is so nice that I would like to have a Mary Jane in my dolls' house too. Keep the house clean for me, Mary Jane, there's a dear."

That night, when the playroom was dark and empty, the little folk in the dolls' house came alive. The mother doll switched on the little electric lights, and the father doll took a stroll outside the house to stretch his legs. The nanny played with the children, and they ran up and down the stairs in delight.

Only little Mary Jane in the kitchen was unhappy. She looked in the dresser cupboard for a broom. She looked in the drawers for a duster. But she couldn't find any at all. So how was she to clean the house, as Joan had said?

She ran to the mother doll and asked her what to do.

"It is dreadful, madam," she said; "there isn't a duster or broom to be found, so how can I keep the house clean for you and the children? Have you any dusters anywhere?"

"No," said the mother doll in dismay. "Well, Mary Jane, my dear, you won't be able to do any cleaning, after all!"

Mary Jane went back to the kitchen and she sat down in the little rocking-chair there and wept big tears on to the floor. What was the good of being a nice little maid doll if she couldn't do any work? She did so want to sweep and dust. It would be fun to keep such a pretty little house clean.

Just as she was feeling most unhappy she heard a little voice calling her. She looked up and saw a pixie peeping in at the kitchen window.

"What's the matter?" he called. "Don't cry! I say, what a dear little house this is! Can I come in?"

"Yes," said Mary Jane, drying her eyes. "But it badly wants sweeping and dusting, and I haven't any brooms or dusters. That's why I'm crying."

"Pooh, you're silly!" said the pixie. "*I'll* get you some!"

With that he ran over to the corner of the playroom where Joan's nanny kept her broom, her dustpan and brush, and her duster. He clapped his hands seven times and sang out a long string of magic words.

And whatever do you think? In the twinkling of an eye the broom, the pan, brush, and the duster all became as small as could be! Mary Jane cried out in delight when she saw the pixie bringing them to her.

"Oh, thank you, thank you!" she said, running to the kitchen door to meet him. "Now I shall be able to do lots of work!"

How happy she was! You should have seen her sweeping all the carpets and dusting all the rooms! How she polished the brass vase in the dining-room and rubbed away at the fire-irons in the drawing-room! She sang as she worked, for she was

proud of being able to keep the house clean.

"You're the best little maid in the world," said the mother doll, delighted. "I think you're just as good as the real Mary Jane, and she's wonderful, because I've heard Joan's mummy say so."

Well, Mary Jane went red with delight. When all her work was finished she put away the duster in the drawer, and the pan, the brush and the broom in the cupboard. Then she went up to her bedroom to go to bed, for she felt tired. Besides, it was nearly cock-crow, and no toys must be alive after that time.

Just after she had fallen asleep the pixie came back for the things he had made small. He knew he must make them big again and put them back where he had found them, for Joan's nanny to use in the morning.

But the dolls' house kitchen door was locked! He banged and banged on it, but it was no good. Nobody opened it. Then he went to the front door and knocked on that. But the father and mother doll had gone to bed and they couldn't hear the knocking upstairs.

Then the pixie tried to get in at the window, but that was shut too. He didn't know what to do. Whatever would the big folk say when they found the broom, brush, pan and duster gone?

At last he gave it up and went away, feeling very upset. Then the cock at the farm cried, "Cock-a-doodle-doo!" and toys and fairies fell asleep everywhere. The real Mary Jane awoke and got up. A little later Joan's nanny also got up. She went to sweep and dust the playroom—and, dear me, she couldn't find the things! How she hunted! Then she asked Mary Jane downstairs if she had taken the things, but Mary Jane said, "No, of course not!"

Well, it *was* a puzzle. Joan's nanny borrowed Mary Jane's things and cleaned the playroom with those. She told Joan's mummy about the strange disappearance of her broom, brush, pan and duster, and Mummy was most astonished.

It was Joan who found out where they had gone. She went to her dolls' house as usual and opened the front of it to see that everyone was all right. How clean the rooms looked! There wasn't a speck of dust anywhere.

Then Joan opened the kitchen cupboard and drawers, for she wanted to lay pieces of white paper on the shelves, just as Mummy did in the kitchen—and she found the broom, the brush and pan, and the duster!

She stared at them in surprise. How did they come there? And what a funny thing! They were exactly like the ones her nanny had, only smaller. Joan took them out and looked at them carefully. Yes, they must be her nanny's! Some fairy must have come along in the night and changed them into tiny ones for the doll

Mary Jane to use—and that was why the house looked so clean and shining!

Joan ran to tell her nanny—but she laughed at her. "Don't be so silly, Joan," she said. "As if I should believe a tale like that! My cleaning-things in the dolls' house! Silly girl! No, I can't come to look. I'm too busy."

Joan went back to the dolls' house. She picked up Mary Jane and spoke to her.

"Listen, little Mary Jane," she said. "I know you have got my nanny's things, but you must give them back. I will buy you a proper little broom, a brush and pan and a duster this morning at the toyshop—but tonight you must see that all the ones you have here are made the right size again. My nanny is very upset because her brushes have gone."

Then Joan took some money out of her money-box and went to buy the things at the toyshop. She bought a fine little broom, a little dustpan and brush, and a tiny check duster. She put them all in the kitchen.

And that night, when the toy dolls woke up again, Mary Jane opened the kitchen door and looked for the pixie. There he was, looking very much worried, for he knew that Joan's nanny had been cross.

"I forgot that those things ought to go back to their place and be made their proper size again," said Mary Jane. "Look, Joan has bought me some toy ones—so please take those others back."

The pixie was glad. He took away the broom, the brush and pan, and the duster, and put them in their right corner. Then he made them big again.

Back he went to the dolls' house, and he helped Mary Jane to clean it from top to bottom with the little new broom, brush and pan, and duster. It was great fun. Mary Jane was very grateful to him.

And in the morning how surprised Joan's nanny was to find all her things in the right place again. She simply couldn't understand it!

"I told you they were in the dolls' house!" said Joan. "You see, I bought the little doll, Mary Jane, a broom, a brush and pan, and a duster, and so she didn't need yours—and here they are back again!"

Joan's nanny didn't believe her. But I do, don't you?

A Surprise for the Wagtails

A pair of wagtails built their nest in some creeper that straggled over a roof. It was a nice nest, and soon it had four little eggs in it.

"Now, I must sit on them to keep them warm," said the hen wagtail. But first she flew off with her mate to catch some of the midges flying in the sunshine.

Whilst she was gone a big cuckoo saw the nest. Now, the cuckoo had made no nest, but she had to have one to put her egg in. So, whilst the wagtails were away, the cuckoo put her egg into their nest, and took out one of the eggs already there. Then she flew off, cuckooing loudly.

The wagtails came back. They didn't notice that one of the eggs was a little larger and not quite the same colour as the others. The hen wagtail sat down to keep them warm. She felt very happy. It is always nice for a bird to feel her warm eggs under her.

Two of the eggs hatched out. One little bird was bigger than the other. He was very bare and black and ugly. He couldn't bear to feel the two eggs near him, nor could he bear to feel the other baby bird pressing against him. When the wagtails had left the nest for a little while, he managed to get one of the eggs on to his back, climbed up to the edge of the nest with it, and tipped it over! Out it went and smashed on the roof.

Then he sank down into the nest, tired out. But it wasn't long before he got the other egg on to his back and tipped that out too!

Then it was the turn of the baby bird. After a lot of struggling the tiny cuckoo got the baby wagtail on to his back, climbed slowly up to the edge of the nest, and tipped him out as well. He squeaked feebly, but no bird seemed to notice him.

Now the baby cuckoo was happy. He had the nest to himself. He settled down and waited for food.

The wagtails were surprised when they found that only one bird was in the nest. "But see how big he is!" they cried. "He seems to grow almost as we look at him. What a fine bird he will be! Finer and bigger than any other wagtail in the garden."

They fed him well. They were very proud of him. They called the other birds to see him. "Did you ever know a finer wagtail baby?" they said. "Isn't he magnificent?"

Soon the baby filled the nest. Then

he was too big for it. He had to stand outside on the roof. He called piercingly all day long, because he was hungry, and soon other birds began to feed him too. Always his big beak seemed to be open!

Then the wagtails had to stand on his shoulders to feed him, for he grew far bigger than they were. How proud they were of him. They talked to the other birds about him, and boasted each day of their marvellous child. They didn't guess that he wasn't their child at all—that he wasn't even a wagtail.

They took him about with them to teach him to feed himself—and one day, what a shock they got! He opened his beak and made a most peculiar noise. They *were* startled.

''He's trying to sing!'' said the wagtails. ''He's trying to say, 'chissic, chissic,' as we do!''

But he wasn't. He was trying to call his first loud ''cuckoo!'' And when he did, what a shock for the poor wagtails!

''Cuckoo! Cuckoo!''

''Oh, he's a cuckoo, he's a cuckoo!'' cried the wagtails.

The other birds laughed. ''We thought he was,'' they said. ''You were a pair of cuckoos, too, to think he was a wagtail!''

The Goblin's Dog

Once upon a time there lived a little boy called Willie. He had a dog named Tinker, and they often went for walks together.

Tinker was fond of Willie, but the little boy was not very kind to his dog. He was supposed to look after him and care for him, but many and many a time he went off to play and forgot all about him.

Tinker lived in a kennel out in the yard. It was a nice kennel, but it needed cleaning out each week. Sometimes Willie remembered, and sometimes he didn't.

Tinker liked fresh water to drink, but often Willie forgot all about his water till it was green and smelt horrid. And, once, poor Tinker had no water at all for two days, because someone had upset it and Willie hadn't noticed.

''Willie, it's cold weather now,'' his mother said to him one day. ''Have you seen that Tinker has plenty of good warm straw in his kennel?''

''Yes, Mother,'' said Willie. But, you know, he hadn't seen—and Tinker had made his old straw so flat that there was no warmth in it at all. So he had to lie and shiver at night when the frost came. He thought of Willie in his warm bed, and how he longed to be able to curl up there with him. But he couldn't, for he was chained up, and had to stay in his icy-cold kennel. It was dreadful.

Now, one night, when Tinker was shivering in his kennel, a small brownie came by on the way to the dairy to get a drink of milk. He heard Tinker shivering, and he popped his head into the kennel.

''What's the matter with *you*?'' he said. ''You seem very cold! Haven't you any warm straw?''

''Not much,'' said Tinker. ''And my water is frozen, too, so that I can't get a drink if I want to. It has been frozen all day. Willie has forgotten to give me any. He didn't take me for a run, either, so I haven't been able to get warm. Do you think you could bring me some water, brownie? There is some in the stream not far away.''

''Certainly,'' said the brownie. He broke the ice in the bowl, emptied it out and ran to the stream. He came back with some water and put it beside the kennel.

"I wish I could get you some straw, too," he said, "but I don't know where there is any."

"Never mind," said Tinker gratefully. "Perhaps Willie will remember tomorrow."

The brownie went to the dairy and had a drink of milk. He was unhappy because he couldn't forget the poor cold dog. He wished and wished he could get some straw. He remembered that a wizard lived not far off, and he thought that maybe he could make straw out of magic. So he went to his house and knocked.

A black cat opened the door, and the brownie went in. Soon he had told the wizard all about Tinker. The wizard listened, and he frowned deeply.

"That boy must be taught a lesson," he said. He clapped his hands, and the black cat appeared. "Fetch the policeman," said the wizard.

The cat disappeared, and when it came back it brought with it a large policeman, with pink wings and a shiny face.

"Go and arrest Willie, who lives at the Farm House," commanded the wizard. "Bring him before the court tomorrow, charged with cruelty to his dog."

The policeman saluted, and disappeared.

And soon, what a shock poor Willie got! He was sound asleep, when he awoke suddenly to find a lantern flashed on his face. The shiny-faced policeman was standing near by, and he spoke sternly to Willie: "Come with me, little boy. I arrest you for being cruel to your dog!"

Willie put on his coat, and went with the policeman. The big policeman suddenly spread his wings and flew through the night, carrying Willie firmly in his arms. There was no escape at all!

The little boy spent the night at the wizard's, and then the next morning the fat policeman took him to a big courthouse. Inside there was a judge, who sat solemnly at a high bench, and had great wings like butterfly wings behind him. There were twelve pixies, brownies, and gnomes sitting at a table below, and there were six policemen, all with pink wings.

"This is Willie," said the policeman who had fetched the little boy. "He is here because of the following things: forgetting to give his dog fresh water—forgetting to give him straw for his kennel—forgetting to take him for a run—and altogether being very unkind."

"Very bad," said the judge, frowning at Willie. "Very bad indeed! Jurymen, what punishment shall he have?"

The twelve pixies, brownies, and gnomes who sat below the judge began to talk excitedly among themselves. Then a long-bearded gnome stood up.

"If you please, your worship," he said to the judge, "we think he should be turned into a dog and sent to one of the goblins."

"Certainly, certainly," said the judge. "A very good idea."

"But you can't do that!" cried poor Willie. "Why, my mother would wonder where I am!"

"Well, we will make your dog Tinker change into *you*," said the judge. "It will be a treat for him to have good food, plenty of fresh water to drink, and a warm bed at night. Now stand still, please, Willie!"

Willie stood still, wondering what was going to happen. The judge took up a wand that lay beside him, leaned over Willie, and tapped him on the shoulder:

"A curious punishment you'll see!
A boy you are—a dog you'll be!"

he chanted. And then he said a very magic word—and, my goodness, Willie found that he was growing black hair all over himself! His clothes disappeared. He grew a long tail. His ears became furry. His nose became long—he had paws instead of hands and feet. He was a little black dog and could only say, "Woof!"

"Take him to the goblin Workalot," commanded the judge.

So Willie was led out of the court on a chain, and taken to a small cottage in a wood. Here a little green goblin lived. He didn't seem at all pleased to see Willie.

"I don't really want a dog," he said to the policeman who brought Willie. "Dogs are a nuisance. But if the judge says I'm to have him I suppose I must!"

There was no kennel for Willie, so he hoped he would sleep on the nice warm rug in front of the kitchen fire. But a big cat suddenly appeared as soon as Willie sat down on the rug.

"Phixxxx-ss-ss-ss!" she hissed at poor Willie. He ran back in fright, and got between the legs of the goblin, who was just coming in with a bowl of water. Down went the goblin, and all the water splashed over Willie.

"Clumsy creature!" cried Workalot. He gave Willie a cuff on the head. Willie hoped he would get a towel and dry him, but he didn't. So the dog sat in a corner and shivered, for he did not dare to go near the fire when the cat was there.

Workalot was a very busy goblin. He ran here and there, he did this and that, and he grumbled and talked to himself all the time. The cat sat and said nothing, but when Workalot needed help with a spell she walked up and sat solemnly in the middle of a big chalk circle.

Soon Willie began to feel very hungry indeed. The cat had a good dinner of fish and milk put down for it, but the goblin did not give Willie any dinner.

"I'll give you something later on!" he grumbled. But he quite forgot, so poor Willie had to go without. He thought he would whine so that Workalot might remember him. But as soon as he began yelping and whining the goblin lost his temper. He took up a big stick and gave Willie a whack with it. Oooh! Willie yelped, put his tail down, and ran under the table. But the goblin pulled him out, took him to the door, and flung him outside.

It was pouring with rain. Willie looked round for shelter, but there was only one bush growing in the garden. He ran to that, and crouched underneath, cold, wet, and hungry. How dreadful it was to be a dog owned by an unkind master with no love in him!

The rain stopped. Willie crept out from the bush, but the door was shut, and he could not get into the house. He looked at the house next door. A dog lived there, too. But it was a dog that somebody loved, for it was well brushed, cheerful, and not at all thin. Willie wished he belonged to a good home too. How lovely it would be to be petted and well looked after!

The door opened and the goblin whistled. Willie ran in. The cat spat at him, and Willie growled back. Workalot gave him a cuff. "Leave my cat alone!" he said. "Go into the corner and lie down."

Willie lay down. The cat sat in front of the warm fire and washed herself. There was an empty bowl not far from her, and Willie felt sure that it had been put down for him—with some meat and biscuits in, perhaps—and the cat had eaten it all up.

Willie fell asleep at last. But when night came the goblin woke him up by

fastening a chain to his collar and dragging him outside. He had put an old barrel there, on its side, and in the barrel he had put a handful of straw. "Get in!" said the goblin. "And mind you bark if the enemy come!"

Poor Willie! He didn't know who the enemy were—and he was frightened to think they might come. He was cold, too, for the wind blew right into his barrel, and he was so thirsty that he would have been glad to lick the snow, if there had been any. He began to whine dismally.

Out flew the goblin in a fine rage, and shouted at him, "Another sound from you and I'll give you the whip!"

After that Willie didn't dare to make another sound. He just lay silent and hoped that the enemy wouldn't come.

Suddenly, at midnight, he heard a little scraping sound at the gate, and he stiffened in fear. The enemy! The gate swung open, and in came—whoever do you think? Why, nobody else but Tinker! He ran up to Willie's kennel and sniffed at him.

"I heard you were here, changed into a dog," he said. "They changed me into you—but I changed back at midnight and I've come to rescue you. You were never very kind to me, Willie, but I love you, and would do anything for you. Now keep still, and I'll gnaw right through your collar."

Willie was full of gratitude to the little dog. He kept still, and very soon Tinker's sharp teeth had bitten right through the leather. He was free!

"Come on," whispered Tinker. "I know the way."

The two dogs sped through the night, and at last came to the Farm House.

"Go up to your room and get into your bed," said Tinker. "In the morning you will be yourself again."

Willie pushed his way into the house and ran up the stairs. He jumped into his warm bed, and was soon asleep. In the morning he was himself.

"It's all very strange," thought Willie to himself, as he dressed. "How kind Tinker was! How awful it is to be a dog belonging to an unkind master. I have been unkind to Tinker often. I never will be again!"

He ran down into the yard. Tinker was in his kennel. He wagged his tail. "Tinker! Tinker!" said Willie, putting his arms round the little dog. "Thank you for rescuing me! I'm sorry I was ever unkind. I will always love you now, and look after you properly!"

And so he did. Tinker has a warm kennel, plenty of fresh water each day, good food, a fine walk in the morning, and lots of pats. He is very happy now—and I do hope your dog is, too!

Chinky Takes a Parcel

Chinky was doing his shopping in the pixie market. It was full today, and there were a great many people to talk to. Chinky was a chatterbox, so he loved talking.

His market-bag was full. He had no more money to spend, and it was getting near his dinner-time. "I really must go home," said Chinky, and he picked up his bag.

"Hi," called Sally Simple, "did you say you were going home? Well, just deliver this parcel to Mrs. Flip's, next door to you, will you? It's for her party this afternoon."

"Certainly," said Chinky, and he took the square box, which felt very cold indeed.

"You are sure you are going straight home?" asked Sally Simple anxiously. "I don't want you to take the parcel unless you are really off home now."

"I'm going this very minute," said Chinky. "Goodbye!"

He set off home—but he hadn't gone far before he met Dame Giggle, and she had a funny story to tell him. He listened and laughed, and then he thought of a *much* funnier story to tell Dame Giggle.

So it was quite ten minutes before he set off home again—and then who should he meet but Old Man Grumble, who stopped him and shook hands. Chinky hadn't seen Old Man Grumble for a long time, and he had a lot of news to tell him. He talked and he talked, and Old Man Grumble hadn't even time to get one grumble in!

"You *are* a chatterbox, Chinky," he said at last. "Goodbye! Perhaps you'll let me get a word in when next we meet."

Chinky set off again. The square cold parcel that he was carrying for Sally Simple seemed to have got very soft and squashy now. It was no longer cold, either. It was rather warm and sticky!

"Goodness! I wonder what's in this parcel?" thought Chinky, hugging it under his arm.

A little drop of yellow juice ran out of one corner and dripped down Chinky's leg. It was ice-cream in the parcel—a big yellow brick of it that Mrs. Flip had ordered for her party. She meant to put it into her freezing-machine when she got it, and then it would keep cold and icy till four o'clock.

Chinky went on his way humming. Some more ice-cream melted and ran down his leg. Chinky didn't know. He was nodding excitedly at little Fairy Long-wings, who was standing at her gate.

"Hallo, Long-wings!" called Chinky. "Glad to see you back. How did you enjoy your holiday?"

And, dear me, he stood talking at Long-wings's gate for ten minutes. Long-wings didn't tell him a word about her holiday, for Chinky was so busy chattering about himself and his garden and his shopping. And all the time the ice-cream dripped down his leg.

Well, when at last he arrived at Mrs. Flip's, the box was almost flat and empty. He handed it to Mrs. Flip, and she looked at it in dismay.

"My ice-cream for the party!" she cried. "It's all melted! Look at your clothes, Chinky—what a mess they are in! Well, really, you might have brought it to me at once! I suppose Sally Simple gave it to you, thinking that you were coming straight home!"

"Well, so I did!" said Chinky indignantly. "I came *straight* home, as straight as could be!"

"I don't believe you," said Mrs. Flip. "I know you, Chinky—the worst chatter-box in town! Oh, yes! You met Mr. So-and-so, and you talked to him for ages, and you saw Mrs. This-and-that, and you chattered for ten minutes, and you came across Dame Such-and-such, and you had a good long talk! And all the time my ice-cream was melting. Take it! I don't want it now—it's just an empty box.''

She threw it at Chinky and it hit him on the nose. He was very angry. He shook his fist at Mrs. Flip and shouted, ''I shan't come to your party now! I just shan't come!''

''Well, don't, then!'' said Mrs. Flip, and she went inside and banged her door. Chinky banged his.

Soon there was the sound of the ringing of a tricycle bell, and along came the ice-cream man. Mrs. Flip heard him and out she ran. She bought the biggest ice-cream brick he had, all pink and yellow. She popped it into her freezing-machine for the party that afternoon.

And when Chinky looked out of his window at half-past four, he saw everyone busy eating ice-creams in Mrs. Flip's garden, as happy as could be.

''Why didn't I go straight home as I said I would? Why did I say I wouldn't go to the party? I talk too much, that's what's the matter with me!'' said poor Chinky.

He was quite right, wasn't he? You would think he had learned his lesson, wouldn't you? But he hadn't. At first, he was quite good, but it wasn't long before he was chattering and gossiping as much as ever. Chatterboxes can't be stopped—easily . . . you try stopping one, and see!

The China Rabbit

On the playroom mantelpiece sat a little china rabbit. It was a dear little thing, with perky ears, a little white bobtail, and two shining black eyes. It was not a toy, but an ornament, and the two children, Anna and Fred, liked it very much. Their mother would not let them play with it in case they broke it.

"You leave it on the mantelpiece and let it look nice there," she said. "It's such a dear little brown rabbit, just exactly like a real one, but much smaller."

So the china rabbit lived on the mantelpiece and was very happy. It watched all that went on out of its shining black eyes. It saw Anna and Fred having their dinner. It saw Anna drop a piece of her pudding on the floor. It heard Mother scold her. It saw Fred put too big a piece of cake in his mouth and choke dreadfully. Mother banged him hard on the back and the cake shot out on the floor.

"Very bad manners," she said crossly, and got the brush and pan. Oh, the china rabbit saw most exciting things, I can tell you.

It saw Fred being stood in the corner for smacking Anna. It saw Anna cutting her pretty hair with the scissors, and, dear me, the china rabbit quite trembled to think what Mother would say to that! Dear, dear, dear, the things the china rabbit had seen happen in the playroom! There was always something to look at.

It saw the toys come alive at night and play happily on the floor. How the china rabbit longed to join them! But it wasn't a toy, so it couldn't. It just sat on the mantelpiece and looked and looked. Sometimes it laughed out loud, because the Teddy Bear was very funny. He put on the dolls' bonnets, and he rode on the clockwork mouse, and sometimes he fell off on purpose and rolled over and over on the floor, knocking down all the watching skittles as he went.

"Do it again!" the little china rabbit would cry. "Do it again!"

The toys were fond of the rabbit. The sailor doll often climbed right up to the mantelpiece to talk to him. The rabbit would listen and listen. But he never left the mantelpiece.

Now, one day a little imp came into the playroom. He came from the mouse-hole, and all the toys stared at him in alarm, for he really was very ugly and very unkind.

He was quick and nimble, and he skipped about everywhere, pulling the dolls' noses, tweaking the toy cat's fine whiskers, tugging at the lamb's tail, and smacking the yellow duck's beak.

Then he saw the pretty little talking-doll hiding away in a corner, for she was very frightened of the imp. The imp stared at her in surprise. He had never seen anyone quite so pretty and dainty. He ran over to her and took her hand.

"Come and live with me in my mousehole," he cried.

But the talking-doll said, "No, no, no!" and ran to the golly for help. Just then the cock crew—it was dawn. The imp had to go, but before he went he shouted: "I'll be back tomorrow. I'll fetch you tomorrow, talking-doll."

The toys were most upset. The next night they hid the baby doll, and where do you suppose they hid her? They hid her behind the big clock on the mantelpiece. It was a very good place. The china rabbit was pleased. He had always liked the pretty little talking-doll. It was nice to have her so close to him.

The golly came up to the mantelpiece too, to take care of her. He sat beside the china rabbit and stroked his ears, telling him all kinds of news.

And then suddenly the imp popped out of the mousehole again. "Here I am!" he cried gleefully, and twisted his long tail about as if he were a cat. "Where's that pretty little doll? She is to come with me!"

Nobody answered. The imp was soon in a rage, for he guessed that she had been hidden. He ran to the brick-box and looked there, flinging out all the bricks. He ran to Mother's work-basket and looked there, throwing out the needles and cottons. He ran to the box of puzzles and looked there—and you should have seen the playroom floor, quite covered with bits of puzzles by the time that imp had finished with the box!

Now, he would never have found the little talking-doll if she hadn't peeped out from behind the clock to see what was going on. As she popped her pretty golden head out, the imp looked up and saw her. "There she is, there she is!" he cried. "I'll soon have her!"

He ran to the chair by the fireplace and began to climb up it. The golly, by the china rabbit, stood up and clenched his fists.

"Throw something at the imp, throw something at the imp!" cried the Teddy Bear from the hearthrug. The golly looked about for something to throw. There were

three pennies on the mantelpiece. He would throw those. He picked one up. Whizz! It flew through the air, but the imp ducked and it missed him. The golly threw another. That missed the imp too, and so did the third penny. The imp climbed steadily up. He would be on the mantelpiece in a moment.

There was a marble on the mantelpiece, too, left there by Fred. Golly picked that up. Whizz! It flew through the air and hit the imp on the foot. He gave a yell of rage and shook his fist at the golly.

"Go on; throw something else!" yelled the toys below. "He's nearly there."

"There's nothing else to throw," shouted back poor Golly. "The clock's too heavy, and so is the moneybox."

"Throw *me*, throw *me*!" cried the china rabbit, suddenly. "Quick, Golly, pick me up and throw *me*! I'll knock him down all right. I'll save the talking-doll."

"But you may break," said the golly.

"Never mind, never mind, just throw me! Oh, quickly, before it's too late!" shouted the rabbit.

So the golly picked up the little china rabbit and hurled him as hard as he could at the imp, who was just about to climb on to the mantelpiece.

The rabbit flew straight for the imp. Crash! It hit him on the head. The imp fell to the ground and lay still. The rabbit fell to the ground too, but—oh, dear!—he smashed into a hundred tiny bits. Wasn't it dreadful? You couldn't tell which bit of him was ear or tail or nose or back—he was all in teeny-weeny scraps on the floor.

The toys were full of alarm. Poor, poor little rabbit! Whatever could they do for him? They picked up all his bits, and put them into a dish from the dolls' house. Then they looked at the imp. He lay in a faint with a great big bump on his head.

The bear fetched some string and tied him up tightly. Then he got a cup of cold water and dashed it over the imp's face. He opened his eyes and tried to get up.

"Oh, no, you don't!" said the golly, giving him a good punch to make him lie down. "You are nicely caught, Imp. You will not be set free in a hurry, I can tell you."

"What was it hit me?" asked the imp, looking round.

"It was the poor china rabbit," said the Teddy Bear, wiping his eyes with his bow. "He was smashed to bits."

"Serve him right," said the imp.

"Oh!" said the golly fiercely. "If you talk like that, Imp, we'll drop you out of the window and see how *you* like being smashed to bits."

"Oh, no, no, no!" cried the imp, in fright. "Don't do that to me. Perhaps I can mend the rabbit for you, I have some magic glue here."

He sat up and they took it from his pocket. It was in a queer long tube. The golly untied the imp's hands, but his legs were still tied.

"If you can mend the rabbit, begin right away," said the golly. "Here are the bits. Put them together and get him right again. You shall not go free till you've finished."

The imp stared at the hundreds of tiny bits in dismay. Then he set to work. He worked all that night—and the next—and the next—and soon the toys saw

the shape of the china rabbit coming again. The imp stuck each tiny bit together in its right place. During the daytime the toys kept him tied up inside the box of the Jack-in-the-Box, and only let him out at night. It was a real punishment for that imp, I can tell you!

At last the china rabbit was quite mended again, though there was one bit over which didn't seem to go anywhere at all. All the glue in the tube was finished. The toys gathered round the rabbit in delight.

''Welcome back, brave little china rabbit,'' they said. ''Can you talk to us?''

The china rabbit found his tongue. It felt rather gluey, but he managed to talk all right.

''How's the talking-doll?'' he asked.

''Quite well, thank you!'' she said, and gave him a big hug. ''Oh, rabbit, it's nice to have you again! It was dreadful when you were all in bits. You shall go back on the mantelpiece again tonight.''

So up he went, carried carefully by the golly, and there he stood once more, beaming down at everyone. As for the imp, he slipped away down the mousehole when no one was looking, but as everyone knew he would be much too frightened to come back again they took no notice.

Fred and Anna were so pleased to see the china rabbit again. They had been very puzzled when he disappeared. They looked at him carefully and saw that he was covered with tiny, tiny cracks.

''Look, Mother,'' said Fred; ''he looks almost as if he had been broken into bits and mended again.''

''Don't be silly,'' said his mother. ''Who would mend him if he broke into tiny bits, I'd like to know?''

The china rabbit stared and stared at the children and longed to tell them who had mended him. But he didn't say a word. He still sits there, as pretty as ever, just beside the clock. You'll see him if ever you go to play with Fred and Anna. Don't forget to look for the tiny, tiny cracks all over him, will you?

Old Mother Wrinkle

Old Mother Wrinkle was a strange old dame. She lived in an oak-tree, which had a small door so closely fitted into its trunk that nobody but Dame Wrinkle could open it. It was opened many times a day by the old dame, for always there seemed to be somebody knocking at her door.

The little folk came to ask her to take away their wrinkles. Fairies never get old as we do—but sometimes, if they are worried about anything, they frown or sulk, and then lines and wrinkles grow in their faces. Frown at yourself in the glass and see the ugly wrinkles you get!

Mother Wrinkle could always take away any wrinkle, no matter how deep it was. She would take a fairy into her round tree-room, sit her down in a chair and look at her closely.

"Ho!" she might say. "You've been feeling cross this week. There's a very nasty wrinkle right in the middle of your forehead. Sit still, please!"

Then she would rub a curious-smelling ointment on the fairy's forehead to loosen the wrinkle. Then she would take up a very fine knife and carefully scrape the wrinkle off. She would powder the fairy's forehead and tell her to go.

"But don't you frown any more," she would call after her. "It's a pity to spoil your pretty face."

Now, Mother Wrinkle had taken wrinkles away for two hundred years, and the inside of her room was getting quite crowded with the wrinkles. She didn't like to throw them away, for she was a careful old dame. She packed them into boxes and piled them one on top of the other.

But soon the boxes reached the top of her room—really, there must be a million wrinkles packed into them. What in the world could Mother Wrinkle do with them?

Now, the fairies did not pay her for taking away their wrinkles. Sometimes they brought her a little pot of honey, sometimes a new shawl made of dandelion fluff—but the old dame hardly ever had any money, and she needed some badly.

"I want a new table," she said, looking at her old worn one. "I would love a rocking-chair to rock myself in when I am tired. And how I would like a pair of soft slippers for my old feet."

She told Sammy, the rabbit, about it one day when he came to bid her good morning. He nodded his long-eared head. "Yes," he said, "you do want some new things, Mother Wrinkle. Well, why don't you sell those boxes of wrinkles and get a little money?"

"Sell the wrinkles?" cried the old dame. "Why, I'd love to—but who would buy them? Nobody! If people want to get rid of wrinkles they certainly wouldn't pay money to buy some. That's a silly idea, Sammy Rabbit!"

The rabbit lolloped off, thinking hard. He liked the old woman. She was always generous and kind. He wished he could help her. He talked to the pixies about it. He spoke to the frogs. He told the hedgehog. He spoke to the bluebell fairy—and last of all he met the little primrose fairy, and told her.

She listened carefully, and then she thought hard. She had been very worried for the last fifty years because the primroses, which were her special care, had been dreadfully spoilt by the rain. Whenever it rained the wet clung to the leaves, ran down to the centre of the plant, and spoilt the pretty yellow flowers. It was such a nuisance. She had been so worried about it that Mother Wrinkle had had to scrape away about twenty wrinkles from her pretty forehead.

But now she had an idea. Suppose she took the wrinkles that the old dame had got in her boxes! Suppose she pressed them into the primrose leaves! Suppose she made them *so* wrinkled that when the rain came the wrinkles acted like little river-beds and drained the water off at once, so that it didn't soak the leaves and spoil the flowers!

"What a good idea that would be!" thought the primrose fairy joyfully. "I'll try it."

So she went to Mother Wrinkle and bought one of the boxes of wrinkles. She took them to her primrose dell and set to work. The primrose leaves, in those days, were as smooth and as thin

as beech leaves—but when the fairy began to press the wrinkles into the leaves, what a difference it made!

One by one the leaves started to change. Instead of looking smooth they looked rough and wrinkled. In the middle of her work the rain came down, and to the fairy's delight the wrinkles acted just as she had hoped—the rain ran into them and trickled to the ground in tiny rivulets!

''Good!'' said the fairy, in delight. ''Now listen, primrose plants! You must grow your leaves in a rosette and point them all outwards and downwards. Then, when the rain comes, your wrinkles will let it all run away on the outside—and your flowers will be kept dry and unspoilt.''

Little by little the fairy gave wrinkles to every primrose plant, and they grew well, till the woods were yellow with the flowers in spring. Mother Wrinkle was delighted to sell the old wrinkles. She bought herself a new table, a fine rocking-chair, and two pairs of soft slippers.

And now you must do something to find out if this strange little story is true. Hunt for the primrose plant—and look at the leaves. You will see the wrinkles there, as sure as can be—delicate and fine—but quite enough to let the rain run away without spoiling the pale and lovely flowers.

Getting Up

I've slept all night through—at last I'm awake,
And out of the window a peep I will take.
What's the day like—is it cloudy or fine?
Is the rain going to pour, or the sun going to shine?

I feel full of beans, though I've not eaten *one*;
I'm ready for shouting and jumping for fun,
I'm hungry for breakfast—oh, what do I smell?
Fried egg and bacon—and sausage as well!

Where are the soap and the towel and the brush,
Where are my vest and my shorts? What a rush!
My slippers have gone—I do think it's queer
The way that my slippers and socks disappear.

I've found them—hurrah!—now I *must* brush my hair,
And fold my pyjamas and put them just there!
I do feel so happy, I'm singing, I'm humming;
There's somebody calling—YES, MUMMY, I'M COMING!

The Adventure of the Toy Ship

Mary and Timothy had a little ship. It had a fine white sail, and its name, *Lucy Ann*, was painted on the side. The children often took it down to the stream to sail it, and it floated beautifully. It didn't turn over on its side, as so many toy boats do—it sailed straight upright, just like a real, proper boat.

One day when Mary and Timothy were sailing the boat the string broke. Oh! Down the stream went the boat, and the children ran after it. But it kept to the middle of the stream, and no matter how they tried, the children could not reach it.

At last they could no longer run by the stream, for a fence stood in their way. So, both very sad, they went back home, afraid that their ship would feel quite lost without them.

So it did. It tried its hardest to go back, but the stream carried it along too strongly. On and on it went, and at last came to rest beside a mossy bank. Its prow stuck into the bank and there it stayed. The little ship could move neither backward nor forward.

Night came, and the ship was astonished to see the Moon in the sky; it had always spent the night in the toy-cupboard, so it did not know there were such things as the Moon or the stars. It stared up at the Moon and thought it was beautiful.

Then it saw on the opposite side of the stream a great many little lights, like Japanese lanterns. It heard a lot of little voices, and saw a great number of fairy folk, all most excited, getting ready for a party.

Toadstools sprang up in a ring, and the pixies laid little white cloths on them for tables. They set out plates and glasses and then put some tiny golden chairs for the musicians to sit on.

The ship watched wonderingly. These must be the fairy folk that Mary and Timothy sometimes talked about. Then it saw a small boat, smaller than itself, on the opposite side of the stream, and a pixie-man getting into it.

Suddenly, quite close by, on the near bank, the ship saw more fairy-folk. They had with them such a lot of good things—honey-cakes, blue jellies with pink ice-cream on the top, lemonade made of dew, fat blancmanges in the shape of birds and animals, and heaps of other lovely things. They carried these goodies in baskets and on dishes, and they were waiting for the boat to fetch them across the stream, so that they might lay out their food on the little toadstool tables.

"Hey! Little boat, come and fetch us!" they cried to the boat on the other side. The pixie-man in it began to row across, but—oh, my goodness me!—suddenly a great fish popped up his head and made such a large wave that the little boat was filled with water, and sank.

Oh, what a noise there was! How all the little folk shouted and cried in fear when they saw their boat sink and the pixie-man in the water!

The little ship suddenly had a grand idea. It would take the pixies to the other side, with all their baskets and dishes. So it spoke in its funny, watery voice, and how all the fairy-folk jumped to hear it! One dropped the dish he was carrying, and spilt jelly all over the grass.

"I will take you across, if you know how to sail me," said the little ship. "Don't be frightened. I am only a toy ship; I cannot hurt you.

I have got lost down the stream, and I will be only too glad to be of any use.''

The pixies ran to it, chattering at the tops of their silvery voices. Yes, the little ship would do beautifully! What luck that it happened to be there! If it hadn't the party would have been spoilt—and the King and Queen themselves were coming!

They all clambered on board and settled down. One of the pixies took the wheel and guided the ship out into the stream. How proud the little toy ship was! Never before had it had anything but dolls aboard, and they could only sit still and stare at the sky. But these little folk chattered and laughed, they ran here and there, they leaned over the side and tried to dip their fingers in the water—it was great fun for the little ship!

Out it went over the stream, sailing most beautifully. The wind filled its sail and it floated like a swan, proud and lovely. The fairies on the other side cried out in delight, and—would you believe it?—at that very moment the King and Queen arrived!

They watched the little boat too, and how pleased they were to see it come safely to the other bank. All the fairies cheered, and the ship shook with joy.

It watched the party go on in the bright moonlight, and saw the little folk dancing as lightly as flies. And then, dear me, what an honour! The King and Queen asked the little ship if it would take them for a sail.

''Oh, Your Majesties, I'd love to,'' said the ship, trembling with joy. ''But the stream is so strong that I find it difficult to sail against it.''

''We will help you by a magic spell,'' said the King. ''You shall take us far up the stream, and when we are tired of sailing we will get into our butterfly-carriage and drive off. Ho, there, pixies, bid our carriage follow us up the stream, so that we may mount it when we are tired of sailing!''

The King and Queen stepped into the boat and off it went, sailing easily against the stream, for the

King used his magic to help the ship. How lovely it was sailing in the moonlight! All the trees were silver, and the little waves on the stream were silver too. Bats flew near by, and the old owl hooted as he flew. It was a most exciting journey.

After a lovely long sail the King spoke to the little ship once more.

"We will land now," he said. "Draw in to the bank, little ship. See where our butterfly carriage awaits us."

The ship saw a lovely carriage drawn by four yellow butterflies. It sailed to the bank and stood there whilst the King and Queen got out. Then it gave a glad cry.

"Oh! This is where Mary and Timothy played with me this morning. Oh, how I hope I can stay here; then they will find me in the morning."

"Of course you shall stay here," said the King. "I will tie you to a stick."

"So he tied the little ship tightly to a stick in the bank, and then said goodbye and thanked the ship very much for its kindness.

"I will turn your sail into a silver one, in reward for your kindness," said the Queen, and in a trice the ship's white sail became one of glittering silver thread. It was really lovely. Then the King and Queen mounted their butterfly carriage and the ship watched them as they went silently away in the moonlight.

Soon it was dawn. The ship slept for a little while, and then woke up. It was proud of its glittering silver sail, and it longed for Mary and Timothy to come down to the stream and see it.

The children came running down before breakfast—and, dear me, how they stared when they saw the little toy ship!

''Look at the beautiful ship!'' cried Mary. ''Where did it come from? It's just like ours was, only it has a silver sail.''

''I wonder who tied it to that stick?'' said Timothy, puzzled. ''Nobody lives here but us.''

''Ooh, look, Timothy—it is our ship! It's called *Lucy Ann*,'' cried Mary in excitement. ''See, its name is on the side, so it must be ours. But how did it get its lovely sail, and who tied it up here for us to find?''

''The fairies must have had a hand in it,'' said Timothy. ''And see, Mary, this proves it. Look at those two tiny cakes on the deck there. The fairies used our ship last night, and one of them dropped those cakes. Did you ever see such things? Shall we eat them?''

''Yes, but let's save them till to-night, and then maybe we'll see fairies!'' cried Mary.

They took their ship from the water and ran to tell Mummy all about it. She was surprised to see its lovely silver sail!

The ship was glad to be back in the toy-cupboard. And how it enjoyed itself telling all its adventures!

Mary and Timothy are going to eat those pixie cakes tonight. I do wonder what will happen, don't you?

The Bear and the Duck

Once upon a time there were two toys, a bear and a duck. They lived on the top shelf in the toyshop, and they had been there for a whole year. Fancy that! A whole year!

They were very unhappy about it. It was dreadful not to be sold. They got dustier and dustier, and at last they almost gave up hope of ever having a little boy or girl to own them.

You see, by some mistake, the duck had a bear's growl and the bear had a duck's quack. It was most upsetting. Whenever the bear was squeezed in his middle, he said "Quack!" very loudly indeed—and whenever the duck was squeezed she said "Grrr-rrrrrr!"

The shopkeeper had tried to sell them, but she couldn't, and that was why she had put them away on the top shelf.

One day a little girl came into the shop with her mother. She was seven years old that day, and she had come to spend the money that her granny had given her for her birthday.

"I want a duck and a bear," she said. Then she pointed up to the shelf. "Oh,

look!'' she said. ''There are two there, and they are just the size I want.''

The shopkeeper took them down from the top shelf—and, oh, how excited the duck and bear felt when they thought they really might be sold to this nice little girl!

''Do they say anything?'' she asked.

''Well,'' said the shopkeeper, ''it's rather funny. The bear quacks like a duck, and the duck growls like a bear. A mistake was made, and it is impossible to put it right.''

The little girl pressed the bear and he made a quack loudly. Then she pressed the duck and it had to growl—grrrr-rrrrrrr!

''Oh,'' said the little girl, disappointed, ''what a pity! I don't like a bear to quack and a duck to growl. It's all wrong. I'm afraid I don't want them.''

The bear and the duck could have cried. The little girl looked at them again, and they looked so sad that she felt sorry for them.

"I'll see if I can get a bear that growls properly and a duck that quacks in the right way somewhere else," she said. "But if I can't—well, I might come back and buy these two."

"Very well," said the shopkeeper, and she put the two toys back on the top shelf again. They watched the little girl take her mother's hand and go out of the shop. They felt most unhappy. To think they could have been sold and gone to the same nursery to live with a nice girl like that.

That night the bear spoke to the duck. "Quack!" he said. "Duck, listen to me. It's quite time we did something to help ourselves."

"Grrr-rrrrrr!" said the duck. "I agree with you. But what can we do?"

"Quack," said the bear, thinking hard. "We will go to the Little Wise Woman

on the hill, and ask for her help. Maybe she can do something for us.''

''Grrr-rrrrr, goodness me!'' said the duck in surprise. ''Dare we?''

''Quack! Certainly!'' said the bear, and he jumped down from the shelf. The duck followed and they went to the window, which was open at the bottom. Out they went, and walked over the wet grass. The duck had to waddle rather than walk, so they couldn't go very fast.

At last they came to the hill where the Little Wise Woman lived. Her cottage was at the top, and the two toys could see that it was lighted up gaily.

''Perhaps she has a party tonight,'' said the duck, out of breath; ''I do hope she hasn't.''

But she had—and just as the two toys got to the cottage the guests began to go. Out went Dame Big-Feet, the witch, on her broomstick, and with her flew her black cat. Out went Mrs. Twinkle, the fat woman who sold balloons all day and made spells at night. After her went Mister Poker-Man, who was as tall and as thin as a poker, and last of all went little Roll-around, who was as round as a ball, and rolled down the hill instead of walking.

''They have nearly gone,'' whispered the duck to the bear. ''Let's wait outside till the cottage is empty.''

So they waited in a corner until all the goodbyes were said, and then they crept out. They peered in at the window, and to their great surprise they saw the Little Wise Woman sitting on a chair, groaning and crying.

''Oh my, oh my!'' she said. ''I'm so tired, and there's all this mess to clear up before I go to bed.''

The bear and the duck couldn't bear to see her so unhappy. They went in at the door, and spoke to the Little Wise Woman.

''We will clear up everything for you,'' said the bear. ''Don't worry. The duck will help you to get to bed, and will make you a nice cup of tea, and give you a hot-water bottle; and I will sweep up the mess, clear the table, and wash up.''

The Little Wise Woman was so surprised that she didn't know what to say.

''Why, you're from the toyshop,'' she said at last. ''However did you manage to get here tonight?''

''Never mind,'' said the bear, determined not to talk about his own troubles now. ''You just get to bed, Little Wise Woman, and go to sleep. We'll do everything else.''

''Grrr-rrrrr!'' growled the duck kindly, much to the Little Wise Woman's surprise.

''Quack!'' said the bear, and surprised her still more. Then she remembered that her friend, the toyshop woman, had told her about a bear who quacked and a duck

who growled, and she thought these must be the two queer toys. How kind they were to come and look after her like this, just when she had so much to do!

The duck took her into the bedroom and helped her to undress. She made a cup of nice hot tea, and gave her a hot-water bottle. Then she tucked her into bed, turned out the light, and left her to go to sleep. The duck was not going to worry the Little Wise Woman about her own troubles now. Not she!

The bear was very busy, too. He cleared all the dirty dishes off the table, and washed them up. He put them neatly away, and swept the floor. Then he put the cakes into their tins and the biscuits into their jars, and put the lids on.

He was very hungry, but of course he didn't dream of taking even half a biscuit. He knew it would be wrong, and he was a very good little bear.

Just as he had finished his work the duck came creeping out of the bedroom.

''She's almost asleep,'' she said in a whisper. ''We'd better go.''

''I'm not quite asleep,'' said the Little Wise Woman, in a drowsy voice. ''Before you go, look in my kitchen drawer. You will find two boxes of pills there. Bear, take a yellow pill. Duck, take a blue one. You won't be sorry you came to help me tonight.''

''Thank you,'' said the bear, astonished.

He knew that the Little Wise Woman had many marvellous spells, and he wondered what would happen when he and the duck swallowed the pills. Perhaps he would grow beautiful whiskers, and maybe the duck would grow a wonderful tail.

He took a yellow pill, and the duck swallowed a blue one. Then they carefully shut the kitchen drawer, called goodnight to the Little Wise Woman and went out into the night.

They were very tired when they got back to the toyshop. They climbed up to their shelf, leaned back against the wall, and fell fast asleep at once.

They didn't wake up until the sun was shining into the shop. The doorbell woke them with a jump and they sat up. They saw the same little girl who had come to the shop the day before. She looked up at their shelf and pointed to them.

"May I see that duck and bear again?" she asked. "I couldn't find any just their size yesterday, so I've come back to see them again."

The shopkeeper lifted them down. The little girl looked at them.

"It *is* a pity the duck growls and the bear quacks," she said.

She pressed the duck in the middle—and to everyone's enormous surprise the duck said "Quack!" very loudly indeed. The most surprised of all was the duck herself. She had never in her life said "Quack", and it felt very funny.

Then the little girl squeezed the bear, and to his joy and astonishment he growled!

"Grrr-rrrrrr!" he went. Just like that.

"What a funny thing," said the little girl. "Yesterday they did just the opposite. Have you had them mended?"

"No," said the shopkeeper, just as surprised as the little girl. "They've not been taken down from their shelf since you went out of the shop. I can't think what has happened to them."

The little girl pressed the bear and the duck again. ''Grrr-rrrrrr!'' growled the bear. ''Quack!'' said the duck. They were both most delighted. So that was what the pills of the Little Wise Woman had done—made their voices perfectly all right. How lovely!

''Well, I will buy them now,'' said the little girl. ''There's nothing wrong with them at all, and they are just what I wanted. I think the bear is lovely and the duck is a dear. I shall love them very much.''

How pleased the two toys were when they heard that! When the shopkeeper popped them into a box, they hugged one another hard—so hard that the duck had to say ''Quack!'' and the bear had to say ''Grrr-rrrrrr!''

''Listen to that!'' said the little girl, laughing. ''They're saying that they're glad to come home with me.''

The duck and the bear are very happy indeed now, and you should just hear the duck say ''Quack!'' and the bear say ''Grrr-rrrrrr!'' whenever the little girl plays with them. They have quite the loudest voices in the playroom.

Twinkle's Fur Coat

There was once an elf who wanted a fur coat. Her friend, Ripple the Pixie, had one, and so had old Goody Tiptap, over the road.

''I want one, too,'' sighed Twinkle the Elf. ''A fur coat looks so nice and keeps people so warm. Ripple, did your fur coat cost very much money to buy?''

''Yes, very much,'' said Ripple. ''It took a whole year's savings.''

''Goody Tiptap, was *your* fur coat expensive to buy?'' asked Twinkle, as Goody came by.

''It belonged to my mother,'' said Goody Tiptap. ''Her brother was a hunter, and he brought home the skins for a coat. I do not know if it would be dear to buy.''

Twinkle counted out her money. She had three pennies and a fifty-pence piece. That was all.

''Certainly not enough to buy a fur coat,'' thought Twinkle sadly.

She put the money back into her moneybox. ''I shan't think any more about a fur coat,'' she said. ''I shall go and call on my Aunt Tabitha, and take her some flowers out of my garden—that is, if I can find any! The poor things are dying because we haven't had any rain for so long.''

She found some flowers and made them into a nice bunch, and set off to her Aunt Tabitha's. On the way there she heard a good deal of squeaking, and she crept through the grass to see what it was all about. She peeped from behind a buttercup—and in a circle of grass she saw a lot of furry caterpillars holding a meeting.

''Good gracious!'' said Twinkle in surprise. ''I never saw caterpillars holding a meeting before. I wonder what it's all about.''

She went to see. The caterpillars turned to her as she spoke.

''Whatever's the matter?'' asked Twinkle.

''Matter enough!'' said the largest furry caterpillar. ''Do you know, all our food-plants are dying for want of rain, and we haven't enough to eat!''

''Really!'' said Twinkle, surprised. ''Well, what are you going to do?''

''We don't know,'' said the caterpillars sadly. ''We could go and find some other

place where the plants are better, perhaps—but we don't know which way to go.''

''What sort of plants do you want?'' asked Twinkle.

''Well, we like plantains and nettles—and lettuce is a big treat, though we hardly ever get it,'' said the biggest caterpillar, waving his black head at Twinkle.

''Now listen,'' said Twinkle. ''I'm going for a walk to my Aunt Tabitha's. On the way I will see if I can find any good food-plants for you to eat. Maybe I can find some in a ditch, where it is damp. I will tell you if I do, and show you the way there.''

''Oh, thank you,'' said the big caterpillar. ''You see, it is nearly time for each of us to change into a chrysalis and sleep, but we do need a good meal first.''

Twinkle set off. All the way to her aunt's she kept a lookout for some nice juicy green plants for the hungry caterpillars—but, alas! everything looked dry and dead. No rain had fallen for three weeks, and the plants were dying.

''Isn't it dreadful?'' thought Twinkle, as she set off back home again. Her aunt was out, so Twinkle just popped into the kitchen and put her flowers in water on the table. ''Isn't it dreadful? No food for the poor caterpillars! All the plantains are dead and dry, and the nettles are grey instead of green! How everything does want rain.''

She came back to the caterpillars. She looked at them sadly and shook her head.

''It's sad,'' she said, ''but everywhere is the same. There isn't a thing for you to eat.''

''Then we shall die,'' said the biggest caterpillar. ''And, oh, what a pity it is, because after one more good feed we should each be ready to turn into a chrysalis, and sleep until we had changed into a beautiful tiger-moth!''

''Oh, do you turn into those lovely red-and-black tiger-moths?'' cried

Twinkle in excitement. "The Fairy Queen has those to ride on when she goes for a moonlight flight! I've seen her—and once she let *me* ride on one of her tiger-moths, and it was lovely! It fluttered its big coloured wings, and up we went in the air."

"Well, I'm afraid the Queen will not have many tiger-moths to ride this year," said the big caterpillar. "If only we could get something green and juicy to eat—but it's no use if you say that everything is dried up."

"Listen!" said Twinkle suddenly. "I will tell you what to do. I have a lettuce-bed, and you shall come with me and eat some of my lettuces. Then you will each be able to turn into a chrysalis, and the Queen will have her tiger-moths to ride on."

"Oh, thank you, Twinkle!" squeaked all the caterpillars. Then, with Twinkle leading the way, they all followed her in a long, furry line, their dark-brown bodies going up and down, up and down, as they walked over the field.

What a feast those caterpillars had in Twinkle's lettuces! Twinkle really was surprised to see how much they could eat. Their jaws opened and shut as they

chewed the green lettuce leaves, and soon there were very, very few lettuces left. Twinkle was rather sad. She hadn't thought that caterpillars could eat so much!

The next day the big caterpillar spoke to her. "Thank you!" he said. "Thank you. Now we shall not eat any more. The time has come for each of us to turn into a chrysalis."

"May I watch you?" asked Twinkle. "It always seems such strange and powerful magic to me when a caterpillar changes into a chrysalis, and then comes out of the chrysalis as a moth or a butterfly! How does your caterpillar body change into a moth's body with lovely big wings, caterpillar?"

"We don't know," said the furry caterpillar. "It is a strange spell, and we don't understand it. Of course you can watch us, little elf. You have been very kind to us. Now, are you ready, caterpillars? Then first of all take off your furry skins! You will not want those in the chrysalis."

So every caterpillar shed its furry coat—and there were all the little furs lying on the ground! The elf suddenly gave a cry of delight, and shouted to the caterpillars: "Don't you want your furry skins any more? Can I have them, please?"

"Of course," said the big caterpillar. "If you don't have them, I expect the mice will come along and eat them, or the beetles. Whatever do you want them for?"

"Ah, you will see when you change into moths and come creeping out of your chrysalises," said Twinkle.

She collected all the furry skins and ran off to the house with them. She washed them well. She hung them on the line to dry. She took her needle and thimble and thread, and she began to sew.

How she sewed! She sewed all those little furry caterpillar skins together, and made a beautiful fur coat from them! You should have seen it! It fitted her beautifully, and was so warm and cosy.

When she had finished the coat, she shook it out and then went to see what had happened to the caterpillars. They were all fast asleep in tight black chrysalis cases! Twinkle touched one—and it wriggled.

"They are alive, but sleeping," said the elf. "How strange that they are growing into moths whilst they sleep! I will wait until they awake—and then I will show them my fur coat."

Weeks later Twinkle went once more to the chrysalis cases, and at the sound of her footsteps the caterpillars awoke, each in his hard little chrysalis case—but they were no longer caterpillars! They had changed magically into magnificent moths—tiger-moths with bright-red, cream, and black wings, beautiful to see!

Twinkle watched each moth make a hole in its case and creep out. Their wings were damp and crumpled—but in an hour or two each moth had dried its lovely wings, and was fluttering them in the air.

"Oh, do you remember me?" cried the elf, dancing up to them. "You knew me when you were furry caterpillars. You gave me your furry skins when you took them off for the last time! Look at the fur coat I made from your skins! Don't you think it is lovely?"

The bright moths looked at her, and waved their feelers about.

"Yes, we remember you," said the biggest moth. "You were the elf who helped us—and we are glad we gave you our skins to make you a fur coat. You deserve it! We will give you a ride, too, any night you want one. You are a kind little thing."

"Thank you!" cried Twinkle.

They spread their wings and flew off to the Queen; but sometimes, when the Queen can spare one of her moths, he flies to Twinkle and gives her a ride through the moonlit wood. She puts on her warm fur coat then, and looks perfectly sweet.

Wasn't it a cheap fur coat? It only cost a few lettuces and a bit of kindness!

The Brownie's Spectacles

There was once a small boy called Billy. He had four brothers and sisters, and all the children lived with their mother and father in a tiny cottage. Their parents were very poor, and Billy could not remember a single Christmas-time when any stocking had been filled, or any birthday when there had been a birthday cake.

The cottage was at the edge of a wood, and the children were forbidden to go there. "It is said that there are brownies and gnomes living in the wood," said their father. "It is best not to go among the trees, for the little folk might take you to work for them."

But Billy did not think the brownies were unkind. He had seen one or two, and he thought their faces were as kind as his father's and mother's. But he was an obedient boy, so he did not go into the wood.

One day he was searching for firewood at the edge of the trees. He had a sack that he was filling with twigs and branches. His mother used the wood for the fire, and it was Billy's job to bring in a sackful each day. He picked up twigs busily, and then stopped to listen. Surely he could hear something?

Yes, he could. It was the sound of someone saying, "Oh, dear, oh, dear, oh, dear!" over and over again! Who could it be?

He soon found out. Behind a tree sat a small brownie with a very sad face, and it was he who was saying, "Oh, dear!" so many times.

"Hallo!" said Billy, coming up. "What's the matter?"

The brownie jumped in fright. "Oh, I didn't hear you coming!" he said. "Look! I've broken my spectacles!"

Billy looked on the ground. There were the brownie's spectacles, smashed to pieces! There was no mending them at all.

"I dropped them off my nose," said the brownie sorrowfully, "and as I am quite blind without them I can't walk another step. So here I must stay until my brother, Longbeard, comes by late this evening. And I have my dinner cooking away in my cottage, and my old grandmother coming to tea. Oh, dear, oh, dear, oh, dear, oh, dear! Oh . . ."

"I've never heard so many 'Oh, dears' in my life," said Billy, laughing. "Cheer up! If you'll tell me the way I'll take you to your cottage. Then you will be able to see to your dinner and give your grandmother tea when she comes."

"Now, that *is* kind of you!" said the brownie gratefully. "I've another pair of glasses at home, so I shall be all right once I get there. Give me your arm, little boy, and I'll tell you the way to go. Go round the big oak-tree to start with—and then between the tall bracken—and then . . ."

Billy guided the little fellow the way he said, and it wasn't long before they arrived at a small blue house set under a great big tree. It had a very large garden indeed, set with tiny trees and nothing else. Not a single flower grew in it.

"Thank you very much indeed," said the brownie, opening the door of the cottage. "Could you look on this top shelf for me and see if you can find my other pair of glasses there?"

Billy found them, and the brownie put them on his nose. "Ah!" he said, delighted. "Now I can see again! Good! Now what about a glass of lemonade?"

"I'd love one," said Billy, "but I'm afraid I mustn't stay. My mother is waiting for her firewood."

"Wait a moment," said the brownie. "I'd just like to give you a present for your kindness."

He ran out of the back door. Billy waited, feeling most excited. A brownie present might be something really wonderful—a sack of gold—a magic purse—a beautiful jewel!

But it wasn't any of those. The brownie came back carrying a small tree that he had just dug out of his garden. It was a tiny fir-tree.

"Here you are," he said. "It's a little Christmas tree. You may find it useful. It's the only thing I can give you."

Billy was dreadfully disappointed. Only a baby fir-tree, the kind he could dig up himself in the wood any day! But he was a polite little boy and he thanked the brownie, said goodbye, and ran off.

When he got home he told his mother of the brownie. She looked at the tree.

"You are foolish, Billy," she said. "You should have asked him for something else. Those brownies know a lot of magic. He might have done you some good. Throw this silly little tree away."

"Oh, I'll plant it in my garden," said Billy. "It's a dear little tree. I may as well keep it."

So he planted it in his garden and then forgot all about it. The summer passed and autumn came. The little tree grew well. Then the autumn passed into cold winter, and the frost and snow came. The little cottage was cold, for the children could not find enough wood to keep a good fire going. There was not enough to eat, either, and when Christmas-time came near, Billy knew it was no use hanging up stockings.

"Father Christmas can't know where we live," he told the others, "and Mother and Father are too poor to buy any presents for us. We must just pretend!"

"Dig up your little tree and let us pretend it is covered with all sorts of presents," said one of the little girls.

So Billy went out and dug up the tree. He put it into a little tub and stood it on the table in the kitchen.

"There you are!" he said to the children. "There's our Christmas tree! We shall have to pretend there are toys on it!"

"There shall be a big doll for me!" cried one little girl.

"And a big book of stories for me!" cried the other.

"A train for me!" shouted Billy's brother.

"Gug-gug-gug!" said the baby, which meant all kinds of things.

"A fat purse for Mother!" said Billy. "And a good pipe and tobacco for Father! And a box of money for me!"

But it was only pretending. There was nothing on the little tree at all. It was very sad.

"Tomorrow is Christmas Eve," said Billy. "I wish Father Christmas would fill our stockings, but I know he won't. Besides, only Baby has stockings this Christmas. We haven't any."

The next night the little tree was put in the kitchen out of the way—but when Billy went to wash up he looked at the tree in surprise. Buds were growing at the end of each little branch. How strange, at this time of year! He looked at it carefully. There was no mistaking it—there *were* buds!

He carried the tree into the kitchen and set it on the table. "Look, Mother,"

he said; "this little tree seems to be budding. Isn't it funny?"

Everyone looked—and, do you know, even as they stared at the tree, they could see the buds growing. Yes, really, they were getting bigger each minute!

Then one of the buds burst—and what do you suppose its flower was? Guess! It was a little red candle! Wasn't that curious? Then another bud burst—and yet another—and they all flowered into candles!

"See this very fat bud!" said Billy, in great excitement. "Whatever can it be going to burst into?"

It certainly was very fat, and it went on growing and growing. It burst at last—and guess what it was! A big doll with curly golden hair, blue eyes, and a pink silk dress! There it hung on the tree, like a big pink blossom. It was the most wonderful and surprising thing that the children had ever seen.

"Mother! It's a magic tree!" cried Billy. "Oh, how glad I am that I didn't throw it away! Just look at it! It's full of buds! I do wonder what they will all be!"

You should have seen that Christmas tree. It was really a wonderful sight. Its buds burst one after another into the loveliest things. There was a train, a book of stories, a pipe, a purse full of money, a box full of coins, a shawl, two pairs of boots, a necklace, a box of soldiers, a pink rabbit, a blue pig, and heaps of other things! The children cut the strange toy flowers off, and as fast as they cut them off more buds grew, burst and became toys or other presents.

"What a wonderful tree!" cried everyone. "We shall have a fine Christmas now!"

"I'm going out to spend some of my money," said Billy. "I'm going to buy a fat goose for tomorrow's dinner, and a Christmas pudding, and lots of sausages, cakes, biscuits, and fruit! Hurray! This will be our first good Christmas!"

Well, it certainly *was* a good Christmas! The little magic tree went on flowering until midnight, and then it stopped—but, dear me, by that time the cottage was quite crammed with good things! It looked as if Father Christmas had emptied twenty sacks there!

"Tomorrow morning I am going to see that brownie who broke his spectacles and thank him very much," said Billy. "I didn't know the tree was such a marvellous one."

So the next day he set off to the little blue cottage. When he got there, what a sight met his eyes! All the little fir-trees in the brownie's garden had flowered in the night, and the ground was covered with all kinds of lovely things. The brownie was busy picking them up and putting them into sacks.

"Hallo!" he said to Billy. "I hope your tree flowered all right."

"Oh, yes, and I've come to say, 'Thank you very much indeed,'" said Billy. "I didn't know it was Christmas trees you grew. I thought it was ordinary trees."

"Dear me, no," said the brownie. "I grow these for Father Christmas. He took about five hundred from me this Christmas. The rest have all flowered, as you see. I am gathering up the toys to send away to children's parties."

"Will my tree flower again next year?" asked Billy.

"Of course!" said the brownie. "It has a Christmas spell in it, you know."

"Oh, how lovely!" said Billy. "I *am* glad I found you when you broke your spectacles that day in the summer, brownie! If you hadn't we wouldn't have had our lovely tree, and all our presents, and our Christmas goose and Christmas pudding and everything! We are *so* happy!"

Off he went—and you can guess what a lovely time he and his brothers and sisters had that Christmas Day. The little tree has been carefully planted in Billy's garden again. He will dig it up next Christmas Eve. Wouldn't you like to see it flowering into toys? I would!

A Fairy Secret

This is an old story which maybe you have heard before—but the secret is such a good one that I am sure you would like to hear it again!

The fairy-folk have very few things to call their own, especially the fairies that live in the flowers. Some of them have an extra shawl to wear on cold nights and some have an extra necklace for a party. But all of them have special dancing-sandals, little goldy ones that shine as they dance at night.

Now the field-mice, whose feet are as tiny as the fairies' own feet, liked to find these goldy sandals and wear them! Then they, too, could dance lightly for hours. So wherever the fairy-folk hid their sandals, the mice hunted them and stole them!

"It's too bad," said the fairies one night when they went to fetch their dancing-shoes from under the violet-leaves where they had hidden them. "Our shoes are all gone again!"

"It's those mice!" said the pixies angrily.

"We shan't be able to dance for weeks now," sighed the elves. "We haven't any money at all to go and buy new sandals from the cobbler."

After a while the little folk had some more shoes made, and very pleased they were with them too, for the cobbler had put tiny buckles on each pair of sandals, with a winking dewdrop for a glittering stone in the middle!

"Those shoes are too precious to be stolen by those naughty little mice!" said the elves, as they tried them on.

"We will hide them at the bottom of a wormhole," said the pixies. So, after the dance that night, that is what they did. They tied their shoes together in a long string and pushed them down to the bottom of an empty wormhole.

But a bright-eyed mouse had seen them and his whiskers twitched with delight. "More shoes! Ha, mouse-feet will go tapping over the fields tomorrow, dancing the Mouse-Walk and the Tail-Parade! I'll go and tell the others."

He ran off. The mice were soon round the hole in the early morning sun, when the fairies were sleeping soundly in the buttercups and other flowers, tired after their night's play.

The mice put down their little front paws and tried to pull up the dancing-sandals. But they couldn't reach far enough down the hole.

"I'll make a burrow from my hole to the wormhole!" said the first mouse, and he scampered down his hole near-by. He soon made a passage to the wormhole, dragged out the shoes into his own burrow and divided them among the small-footed mice. How grand they looked in their tip-tapping golden sandals!

But the fairies were very sad when they found that their new shoes had been stolen. They hunted for them everywhere, but the mice had hidden them well and they never found them again.

"It's no use our buying new shoes and having them stolen each time like this," said the pixies.

"Then we must find some really good hiding-place!" said the fairies. "And we will put a spell on our shoes now, so that if anyone drags them from their hiding-place they will no longer be shoes!"

So they hunted and hunted to find a good place.

"The bottom of the poppies would be good," said a pixie. "We could cover the shoes with the black stamens."

"That would make them so black, though," said an elf. "No, that won't do. What about inside a foxglove bell?"

"Silly idea!" said the fairies at once. "The bumblebees go there every day, and they would buzz the news all round at once if they found our shoes tucked away near the nectar at the back. Think again, elf."

So the elf thought again—and this time she thought of a really good hiding-place, where she was sure the mice would never look. So all the little folk hid their shoes there after the next dance—and they put a spell on them too, so that the sandals would change into something else if anyone took them!

The mice hunted everywhere. They sniffed inside the buttercups, they blacked their noses by looking in the sooty middle of the poppies, they

hunted in every wormhole they could find, making the worms very angry indeed.

But they couldn't find them! Not one sandal could they see, and they haven't discovered the fairies' secret yet!

Would you like to know it? Well, I'll tell you—but don't try to take the sandals, will you, for they certainly won't *be* fairy dancing-shoes any longer if you pull them away from their hiding-place!

If you want to see them, go and hunt for the big white dead-nettle flowers that grow everywhere by the fields and hedges and waysides. Look inside the flowers, but look in the *top* of the flower, not the bottom—and there, neatly arranged in their pairs, you will see the hidden goldy sandals of the little folk!

Isn't it a good hiding-place? Touch the little shoes gently, and maybe they will leave magic in your finger that will bring you good luck all that day!